Virtuosi

A DEFENSE AND A (SOMETIMES
EROTIC) CELEBRATION OF GREAT PIANISTS

MARK MITCHELL

INDIANA UNIVERSITY PRESS

Bloomington and Indianapolis

This book is a publication of
Indiana University Press
601 North Morton Street
Bloomington, IN 47404-3797 USA
http://www.indiana.edu/~iupress
Telephone orders 800-842-6796
Fax orders 812-855-7931
Orders by e-mail iuporder@indiana.edu

Library of Congress Cataloging-in-Publication Data

Mitchell, Mark (Mark Lindsey)
Virtuosi : a defense and a (sometimes erotic) celebration of great
pianists / Mark Mitchell.
p. cm.
Includes bibliographical references and index.
ISBN 0-253-33757-7 (cl : alk. paper)
1. Piano—Performance. 2. Pianists. 3. Virtuosity in music. I. Title.

ML700 .M57 2000
786.2'193—dc21

00-038897

1 2 3 4 5   05 04 03 02 01 00

FOR

David Leavitt

There is no greater consolation for mediocrity than that genius is not immortal.

—*Goethe*, ELECTIVE AFFINITIES (*1809*)

It raises the spirits somewhat like champagne, but better than champagne, and it has all the arrogance and costly unreason that are so fascinating in fine jewellery, in common with which it seems to convey a kind of magnificent protest against matter-of-fact and gloom.

—*Arthur Johnstone, from a review of a concert by virtuoso Moritz Moszkowski (Manchester, 18 November 1898)*

Neurotics are the torchbearers of civilization.

—*Ernest Jones*

Contents

From the Green Room

This book was born, quite frankly, from a frustration with traditional writing about music. Virtuosity and the virtuoso have been discounted too routinely—largely due to the conservatism of music critics and musicologists. I offer this testament as *un amateur* who has long wanted a direct and informed consideration of expressive material without, as one scholar puts it, "having to go through all the nonsensical private language and dangerous anticreative agendas that have bedeviled so much contemporary scholarship."

It is, of course, impossible to be comprehensive, and a number of superb artists are not represented in these pages. If I do not sing of Guiomar Novaës (whom many in her audiences regarded as the greatest of pianists), it is because I never had the opportunity to hear her—and not because I fail to admire some of her recordings. (I admire particularly her recordings of Mozart's "Jeunehomme" and D minor concertos with Hans Swarowsky.) If I speak more about concerts I have attended than about great recordings, it is because my experiences of the former have made me distrustful of the latter.

I have felt torn between underplaying and emphasizing the subjective nature of my endeavor. In the end, I must revel in it— this is a personal celebration of the virtuoso, with some fisticuffs (on the virtuoso's behalf) along the way. Here I hope one will hear the spirit of virtuosity itself: adrenaline, perversity, nostalgia, the personal and the expressive, and above all, a pervasive love.

Virtuosi

THE LESS FRACTIONED WORLD

My dad's parents had lived in that house since they married, and at first they shared it with his parents. My grandfather's grandfather built the house no later than the 1880s (no one knows the exact date): wood, with high ceilings, four fireplaces, and porch all along the front. In those days it was fairly primitive: the only modern features were electricity, gas heat, and indoor plumbing. Still, there was a well behind the house, under the pecan trees, and in the summer I would take my bath outside in a galvanized steel tub filled with water drawn from this well; water sweet, yet tasting also of iron. Those nights were deeply fragrant, but two smells of the house emerge into memory as well: one of towels dried on the clothesline, the other of witch hazel. Considering that my grandmother was, finally, constrained by shame of the body, I wonder that I experienced such an almost pagan rite as these baths at her house, in her back yard. They were a sublimity of twilight and water and nakedness and heat and fireflies and the distant sound of the television.

The house itself was gloomy and haunted. The century was present in it, in great ways and small ones: the downward motion of the glass in the six-over-six windows; a bit of the wood ceiling in the hall that was charred from where there was a fire in the attic in the twenties; the white-on-white fern-patterned wallpaper in the living room that was evidence of the vogue for monochrome decor after the Second World War; a *National Geographic* map from the fifties representing a world less fractioned than ours. There were two iron-framed beds in the guest bedroom, and one of these, the one my brother and I slept in when we visited, was pushed against the front of the piano: an Adam Stoddard rectangular grand, the case rosewood and *ante-bellum* (ca. 1850s), the ivory keys yellowed and fewer than eighty-eight in number, the ebony ones faded to the color of old widow's weeds. My grandmother had long before taken the claw-foot piano stool into her sewing room, since its height could be adjusted for comfort. I had to sit on the bed when I tried the instrument, but this was the smallest of challenges. The piano, like purgatory, had worlds above and beneath it: a first-generation vacuum cleaner, a battered Hartmann leather trunk full of a great aunt's formal clothes, and a paper grocery bag of spent spools reposed around the lyre of the pedals; a broken lamp, issues and issues of *Modern Maturity* magazine and some plastic- and flocking-poinsettias my mother had given my grandmother one Christmas were ranged across the lid.

The day I first tried the piano was cold—outdoor baths were a memory—and therefore the bedroom was closed off: only a run of rooms could be kept warm by the gas heaters, the asbestos panels of which glowed blue and vermilion and gold like the stained-glass windows of a cathedral—or so I thought as a boy disposed to poetry. I could see my breath, and half-imagined, half-hoped, that each key, depending upon how I struck it, might issue up a puff of the visible. This did not happen, alas, but because the room was cold the notes really rang out.

There were few classical records around our house during my boyhood: Tchaikovsky's *Romeo and Juliet*, Stravinsky's *Rite of Spring*, a Beethoven fifth symphony pressed on red vinyl, Mozart's piano quartets, Rubinstein playing Chopin, a three-disc Beethoven set that included Serkin playing the "Moonlight," *Pathétique* and "Appassionata" sonatas and the fifth concerto. My parents came of age in the sixties, and though they liked classical music well enough, they preferred Joan Baez and Jackson Browne and Bob Dylan, The Incredible String Band, Joni Mitchell and Jesse Colin Young. As it happened, my own interest in classical music was kindled by a Band-Aid commercial in which a boy played the opening of Grieg's A minor piano concerto. Through it all, the Band-Aid stayed on. (The first classical record I bought was a 1959 Lisztian performance of this concerto by Kjell Bäkkelund

with Odd Günther-Hegge and the Oslo Philharmonic Orchestra.[1])
My interest was fanned into flame, however, a few days after
Christmas of 1977. On I-75, near Gainesville, Florida, I heard on
the car radio the "Moonlight" sonata and realized that this was
what I had been waiting for. This day also marked the beginning
of the end of our Serkin recording of the sonata (which I had
never before listened to), for I played it until it was worn smooth.

Two years later—on 20 December 1979—I attended my first
classical concert: a recital by the Catalan pianist Alicia de Larrocha in West Palm Beach. She played Beethoven's opus 33 bagatelles, Bach's second *English* suite, the Bach-Busoni *Chaconne,* Schumann's opus 8 *Allegro,* and Ravel's *Gaspard de la nuit.* Among the
encores was de Falla's *Ritual Fire Dance* ("To chase away the Evil
Spirits"). My dad took me to the concert, in our temperamental
Fiat, and picked me up afterwards.

No, I am wrong: the first classical concert I attended was a Sunday afternoon piano recital at the Gallery Fantasia—a monument
to the work, much of it stained glass, by an artist named Conrad
Pickle—in Boynton Beach, Florida (a building later converted
into office space and now sadly untended). The pianist, whose
name I do not recall, played Scriabin's fifth sonata and Gershwin's
Rhapsody in Blue.

---

1. Grieg's was the first piano concerto recorded, in 1909. Wilhelm Backhaus
was the soloist.

1.

The Triumph of Marsyas

Marsyas, a satyr of Phrygia, who, having found the
flute which Athena had thrown away in disgust on
account of its distorting her features, discovered
that it emitted of its own accord the most beautiful
strains. Elated by his success, Marsyas was rash
enough to challenge Apollo to a musical contest,
the conditions of which were that the victor should
do what he pleased with the vanquished. Apollo
played upon the cithara, and Marsyas upon the
flute. The Muses, who were the umpires, decided
in favour of Apollo. As a just punishment for the
presumption of Marsyas, Apollo bound him to a
tree, and flayed him alive. His blood was the
source of the river Marsyas, and Apollo hung up
his skin in the cave out of which that river flows.

—*E. H. Blakeney and Sir William Smith*

Something there is that does not love a virtuoso, and the word
itself has often been applied dismissively, as an accusation of
superficiality. Although critics have been the most open, if un-
systematic, vilifiers of the virtuoso, some musicologists have
been no less culpable. Indeed, the growing institutionalization of
Western classical music since the Second World War has owed
primarily to the influence of musicologists and scholarly performers—"the academy," for want of a more precise or poetic
term. Joseph Kerman identifies his archetypal musicologists as
coming "from the middle class; they are indeed likely to be moving up within its spectrum. It is middle-class values that they

project and seek to protect. . . ." In such circles, doing a thing competently is generally better than doing it passionately: passion doesn't pay the mortgage. In counterpoint to anti-virtuoso elements in the academy, there exists a pro-virtuoso establishment, for which a primary forum is *The International Piano Quarterly* (the *IPQ*), devoted chiefly to the history and comparison of recordings, to biographies of obscure pianists (Robert Lortat, Noel Mewton-Wood, Walter Rummel, Leo Sirota, and Ignace Tiegerman, for example), and to "appreciations" of the unassailable. Bringing to light the stories of virtuosi who have fallen into neglect is ever an estimable pursuit. The decision to focus so relentlessly on their recordings, however, seems to me deeply flawed. Liszt, of course, did not leave us a single recording. Other virtuosi, captured on cylinder or disc when the phonograph was young and they were old, made recordings that do not reflect their glory. Still others have been allergic to the artificial performance conditions of the recording studio. Above all, technically massaged recordings tell us little about actual performances. Radu Lupu, for example, made a magnificent recording of Schubert's A minor sonata, D. 784, yet each of the half dozen times I have heard him in concert he has disappointed and frustrated me. On one program were Schumann's *Davidsbündlertänze*—a composition about which the composer had written to Clara (this was before they married), "[I]f I was ever happy at the piano, then it was as I was composing these dances." Lupu's interpretation, on the other hand, had none of the ardor, none of the tentativeness and rambunctiousness, of a young man full of wedding thoughts—or eager to dance with comrades determined to overthrow the Philistines. Indeed, the only mood, or personality, Lupu cultivated was stoniness (*sans* David's sling). Which, then, tells the truth—the recording or the concert?

This parallel, pro-virtuoso establishment often seems more concerned with uncovering rarities *per se*, or simply being perverse, than with locating recordings that exemplify an important aspect of the virtuoso tradition. For example, in a recent survey of all complete recordings of the Chopin *études* published in the *IPQ*, Donald Manildi gave pride of place not to Pollini or even Cortot (whose first recording tied for second with Ashkenazy's first recording) but rather to the Cuban-American pianist Juana Zayas. (A number of audible edits on her recording suggest technical insecurity.) In the same vein, a piano historian friend rebuked me for "showing a lack of historical comprehension" about the English piano tradition because I was not familiar with the playing of Katharine Goodson, in his view the greatest of all English pianists—greater than Curzon (whose teacher she was), greater than Hess, greater than Solomon. He did concede, however, that as Goodson made no recordings, and only a single tape of her playing exists, I would have been hard pressed ever to hear her. In such situations, the quality of the playing seems to matter less than the pride of discovery.

In *Exiled in Paradise*, Anthony Heilbut argues that

> art history and musicology were invaded, if not invented, by émigré scholars. Musicologists joked that Arnold Schoenberg had made their discipline a viable one, the extreme difficulty of his theories having convinced American educators that anything so abstruse must be academically respectable.

In the subsequent half a century the academy has increased its influence, and the abstruse has remained a principle of music writing to the present day. The academy has separated itself from "musical insights and passions" (Kerman). In partial consequence, criticism of the virtuoso has gained a foundation in— indeed, the support of—the academy.

Musicologists are as heterodox as any other body of people who have only their trade in common. Pieter C. Van den Toorn's *Music, Politics, and the Academy* contrasts positivist and formalist methods of study with the interdisciplinary ones of the "New Musicologists" such as Kerman, Leo Treitler, and Susan McClary (whose sexual politics lead to what Van den Toorn diagnoses as a *"musicology of resentment—personal resentment"*). Despite Van den Toorn's complaint that the New Musicologists are too ideological, he himself argues against them from a highly conservative—and ideological—position: his dogged analysis of Beethoven, for instance, privileges formalism over McClary's feminist interpretation. Van den Toorn argues that this kind of analysis, which Bernard Shaw famously lampooned, permits of the deepest intimacy with the musical text; yet this intimacy, notwithstanding how much it means to its practitioner, is not expressive. Instead, it is description—and turgid description at that.

"Virtuoso" referred to the learnèd in general, and especially in the physical sciences it would seem, for some time before the term settled on musicians. The *Dictionnaire de Musique* by Sébastien de Brossard (1703) marks a stage in this evolution:

> *Virtù* means, in Italian, not only that propensity of the soul which renders us agreeable to God and makes us act according to the rules of right reason; but also that superiority of talent, skill, or ability which makes us excel, be it in the theory or be it in the practice of the Fine Arts, beyond those who apply themselves as much as we do. It is from this word that the Italians have formed the adjectives *virtuoso* or *virtudioso*, to name or praise those to whom Providence has granted this excellence or superiority. . . .

By the early twentieth century, we can find the following:

> *Virtuoso.* One who is remarkably skilled in performing on some special instrument. Virtuosos are constantly tempted to indulge in an undue exhibition of their wonderful technic, and as many have succumbed to the temptation, the term virtuoso has come to be considered by many as slightly depreciatory, and the greatest artists usually object to having it coupled with their names. (W. L. Hubbard et al., 1908)

Today's critical representation of the virtuoso is startlingly narrower than Bossuet's, precisely because it divorces "right reason" from technical excellence. The academy's favored "virtuoso" has the technique to be reliable and "get the job done," but has no need for transcendent technical ability, while it regards the Romantic virtuoso as lacking in right reason.

Marsyas, a satyr, becomes a virtuoso player of the flute that Athena has cast away. Lyre-playing Apollo, jealous of the satyr's virtuosity and public success, challenges him to a musical contest which will be judged by the Muses. In the end, Apollo triumphs—not because he is the better musician, but because he set Marsyas the task of playing and singing at the same time, as he himself has; an impossibility for a flute player. Apollo punishes Marsyas by flaying him alive and nailing his skin to a pine.

(As with any bit of gossip, individual accounts vary on the details.)

In the fourth chapter of his *Republic*, Plato came down on the side of Apollo and his lyre, because Marsyas's *aulos* made music that was too dangerous and disquieting—too virtuosic—for the state to tolerate. Perhaps we should not be surprised, since Plato was the father of the academy. Adorno knew that great music surpasses in scale of importance the modes and occasions Plato had assigned to it: great music—as from the *aulos* of Marsyas, who was less than human and more than divine—reminds the dehumanized masses of their humanity.

The musician capable of achieving all that he sets out to do threatens the academy, for true genius defies all attempts to measure, to constrain, to define it. In *A Room with a View* Forster writes,

> The kingdom of music is not the kingdom of this world; it will accept those whom breeding and intellect and culture have alike rejected. The commonplace person begins to play, and shoots into the empyrean without effort, whilst we look up, marvelling how he has escaped us. . . .

In the presence of the virtuoso, one either marvels with Forster, or chafes at being left behind. The academy takes the latter tack. For while Oscar Wilde was unafraid to call the critic an artist—Walter Pater on Leonardo da Vinci illustrates the point—the fact remains that few critics have ever produced the sort of criticism that Wilde called "the record of one's own soul." Accordingly, musicians whose interpretations are the record of a fine and unique soul tend not to be embraced as readily as those whose performances are accepted as "straightforward" *explications de texte*—even though the *explication de texte* is hopelessly *démodée* as a method of academic discourse.

When Schlegel asserted that "[e]xcellent works generally criticize themselves," he seemed almost to anticipate Wilde's age of secondary texts. The point is a keen one, yet it is not applicable to music because the ordinary person cannot from looking at a score determine how it will sound: for this ordinary person, *Augenmusik* does not exist, and the score of Berg's *Wozzeck* cannot be read the way *Nicholas Nickleby* can. George Steiner (in *Real Pres-*

ences) extends Wilde's thesis by putting forward the interpreter
himself as critic:

> Each performance of a dramatic text or a musical score is a cri-
> tique in the most vital sense of the term: it is an act of penetra-
> tive response which makes sense sensible.... Unlike the re-
> viewer, the literary critic, the academic vivisector and judge,
> the executant invests his own being in the process of interpre-
> tation . . . in respect of meaning and of valuation in the arts, our
> master intelligencers are the performers.

The virtuoso, in short, is not a re-creator but a collaborator
with the composer: the performer and the music dwell in sym-
biosis. No theoretical analysis or musicological investigation can
critique Beethoven's C minor piano sonata, opus 111 more elo-
quently and comprehensively than a magnificent performance of
it, which, as Peter Kivy argues, is the "ultimate nonverbal description of the work." (He could easily have omitted "nonverbal.") No study of the *clavecinistes* is more acute than Debussy's
piano music; no study of the slow movement of Mozart's clarinet
quintet will prove more penetrating than the *adagio* of Ravel's G
major piano concerto. (Few who see music "as their own most
private concern"—as did Furtwängler, conductor of the Berlin
Philharmonic from 1922 to 1954—would agree with Edward W.
Said, who adjudged that the critical essay and the musical performance are interpretive presentations "almost of coeval interest
and worth.") While the reading of a paper at a scholarly confer-
ence may be followed by polite and even heartfelt applause, I
have heard thousands of people become hysterical after Krystian
Zimerman played Chopin's B-flat minor sonata and Kissin played
Liszt's "La Campanella."[1] The superiority of Kissin and Zimerman to Said rests in the fact that they are not only players, but *virtuosi*. This is not a response based on a susceptibility to glamour
at the expense of allegedly more profound interpretive gifts. Still,
when Wilde proposed that only superficial people do not judge
by appearances, he touched on a truth: the authentic virtuoso's
performance transforms our feelings, the life of our senses, into
knowledge.

1. Backhaus demanded that a virtuoso have this piece always available, and
he himself played it as the last work of no less important and celebratory an occasion than his twenty-fifth recital in London.

Italian novelist, critic and film director Mario Soldati, in an essay titled "La sorpresa di un verde-chartreuse," wrote that ours is a sad age because it has no great living musician: the last, he believed, was Stravinsky (who died in 1971). Pianistically, our age is not so sad, though it is at best a bronze age. Indeed, one may argue that three of the most highly regarded pianists of the present moment—Brendel, Lupu, and Perahia—are not *virtuosi* in the golden Romantic sense; moreover, with (in my concert-going experience) the one-time exception of the second of them[2] and the occasional exception of the third, they do not play the most "pianistic" of piano music (that of Alkan, Chopin, Debussy, Liszt, Medtner, Ravel, Rachmaninov, Schumann, and Scriabin). To be praised for playing the piano with intelligence, lyricism, and warmth—as these pianists commonly are—is an achievement, yet these qualities may be regarded as shortcomings as well, taking the place of the virtuoso's instinct and intuition, of his heat (and, sometimes equally, his *froideur*). "Brains and brimstone" (the phrase is Shaw's) are not mutually exclusive. Brendel, Lupu, and Perahia keep within middle-class bounds (whether by design or default is arguable), and thus they are the Apollo, not the Marsyas, of the piano world.

No virtuoso pianist of this century has been regarded by most as *the* Beethoven pianist, though Liszt, the nineteenth-century's *virtuoso assoluto*, was regarded also as its supreme interpreter of Beethoven. (Beethoven was the ideal of a musician in the Romantic era; the very embodiment of Hegel's passionate man of genius.) Like Schnabel before him, and Liszt's Scottish pupil Frederic Lamond[3] before *him*, Brendel—notwithstanding an ample harvest of blunt, dull, and pedantic Beethoven concert performances and recordings—is held to be the finest Beethoven interpreter of our day. Yet Joachim Kaiser, writing in the 1960s,

---

2. The works on the first half of Lupu's 5 December 1998 recital in Florence were Ravel's *Pavane pour une Infante Défunte* and *Sonatine*, Gershwin's three preludes, and Debussy's *Estampes*. The second half was devoted to Brahms's F minor sonata, opus 5. Janácek's *Sonata 1.X.1905* appeared on his programs during this same season.

3. The program from an all-Beethoven recital—the *Hammerklavier, Andante favori, Pathétique*, rondo opus 51, no. 2 and "Appassionata"—given by Lamond at Wigmore Hall (London) describes him as "The Greatest Living Exponent of Beethoven." He was, moreover, the first to record Beethoven's E-flat concerto.

held that "No supposed 'Beethoven specialist' is [Rubinstein's] superior." Though Brendel has developed as a Beethoven player in the last three decades and is, by any standard, a fine pianist, in my view (but not mine alone) his Beethoven playing has not surpassed Arthur Rubinstein's—or, for that matter, Arrau's, Gilels's (which I seem to be just about alone in admiring), Kempff's, Kovacevich's, Pollini's, Rudolf Serkin's (his performance of the opus 110 sonata was one of the most transformative experiences of my life), or Sofronitsky's (he was the supreme interpreter of the *Pastorale* sonata). One of the desert-island discs chosen by the late Isaiah Berlin was a recording of a late Beethoven string quartet played by the Busch Quartet—a performance he loved because it was not virtuosic (a term, for him, of real disapproval). Perhaps, for the same reason, Brendel was the contemporary pianist most admired by Berlin—the same Berlin who in 1965 gave a series of lectures celebrating the movement that signaled the end of the sovereignty of the Rationalist tradition: Romanticism.

As unfashionable as it may be, I regard Brendel as English composer and critic Kaikhosru Shapurji Sorabji regarded Schnabel:

> Each fresh hearing of this pianist leaves me more and more astonished at his almost legendary reputation with the wiseacres, the art-snobs, the fashionable sedulous apes who monkey the latest cackle, and with certain otherwise intelligent music-lovers. . . . The wiseacres naturally admire a dull and dreary imagination—and, soulless pedant, he is a mirror wherein themselves are reflected, a man of the commentator tribe . . . the intelligent music-lovers surprise one more than all the rest by their inability to see through all this pretentious mock-profundity, this Day-of-Judgment tone of voice when saying 'It's a nice day.'

The celebration of Brendel insults intellectualism by stripping it of its capacity to elate and to incite wonder (Pollini, in this regard, is a true intellectual); insults the Romantic virtuoso by painting him as mindless (that is, less an exponent of mind over manner than the reverse); and insults Beethoven's music by holding that this one performer, perhaps alone among living pianists, has its secret. One French critic actually lauded Brendel's third *intégrale* of the concerti because "Beethoven est là, tout Beethoven, et Beethoven seul."

Shortly after he had finished recording his third Beethoven sonata cycle, I heard Brendel play the last three sonatas; a sort of program, not incidentally, that Wagner considered utterly inappropriate for a reason that will be explained shortly. One of our most perceptive and musically literate writers (of whom also more later) went to this concert with me—which happened to be the first time I heard Brendel play Beethoven sonatas since his Beethoven sonata cycle at Carnegie Hall in 1983—and afterwards spoke of the cult that surrounds this pianist (for he is, unarguably, a cult pianist): the writer's feeling was that he was hearing less a performance of Beethoven sonatas than a lecture on Beethoven sonatas: articulate, literal, uniform, occasionally sensitive, but for all that, still only a lecture.[4]

Gregor Benko describes Brendel's reaction to hearing Hofmann play Beethoven's opus 31, no. 3 sonata:

> An interesting personal experience touches on the question of Hofmann's Beethoven: in the early 1970s, before this recording had been reissued, pianist Alfred Brendel visited me in my New York office, having learned of the recording's existence. He was eager to hear it and approached the listening session with respect and anticipation. Delight and amazement were visible on his face as he listened—until a certain spot where Hofmann deviated minutely from the printed page. "Stop!" exclaimed Brendel, and he refused to hear another note, explaining to me, "That one deviation negates the whole performance for me—I don't want to hear it."

By contrast, from the first notes of the Chopin F major ballade that Kissin played in concert, there was no doubt that he was a virtuoso; that he was playing the work better than any pianist before him because he respected and fulfilled Chopin's enormous demands with passion and poetry and a stupendous technique. (The *agitato* section was absolutely terrifying—much more so than on his recording.) Kissin's playing—the playing of the virtuoso—answers Pater's call to experience itself, whereas Brendel's cultivates the fruits of experience. It was Eliot for whom

---

4. Brendel marked the fiftieth anniversary of his professional début (1948 in Graz, Austria), with a recital in London. His playing of Mozart and Schubert was handsome enough, but in Haydn's E-flat major sonata he pressed the humor to the point of caricature. After his encore (the second movement of Mozart's A minor sonata, K. 310) he was presented with rare bottle of 1948 Armagnac.

"The knowledge derived from experience [had] . . . / At best, only a limited value": "The knowledge imposes a pattern, and falsifies, / For the pattern is new in every moment / And every moment is a new and shocking / Valuation of all we have been" (*Four Quartets:* "East Coker" II).

This must be writ large: virtuosity is not uneasy when faced with academic realities, with scholarly expertise, with the achievements of those who play differently. (Horowitz admired Backhaus and Serkin—he often played duets with the latter. To be faithful to one's own vision does not preclude sympathy with that of another.) The academic *system*, on the other hand, *is* often uneasy when faced with the transcendent musicianship that defines virtuosity: it is the menace against which its wagons must be circled. Mark Edmundson, in an essay titled "On the Uses of a Liberal Education," quotes Northrop Frye: "The artist who uses the same energy and genius that Homer and Isaiah had will find that he not only lives in the same palace of art as Homer and Isaiah, but lives in it at the same time." Edmundson's wistful observation that this sentence is "now dramatically unfashionable" further testifies to the stifling hegemony of the academy.

In a larger sense, things of astounding beauty, of perfection, are daunting, intimidating, uncomfortable. This is why Dorothea, confronted with the "weight of unintelligible Rome," weeps in her room in Eliot's *Middlemarch.*

Liszt was the first really great virtuoso pianist, as well as the fountainhead of modern piano technique. Saint-Saëns, in his *Portraits et souvenirs,* offered Liszt the supreme compliment when he wrote, "The remembrance of his playing consoles me for being no longer young." Liszt played not only his own music, but all the best music that had been written for the instrument until his day—and this is to say nothing of his pioneering achievement as a conductor; a catholicity few enough present-day *virtuosi* exhibit. Thus, in addition to playing the music of Bach, Händel, and Scarlatti, Chopin, Hummel, Mendelssohn-Bartholdy, Schumann, and Weber, Liszt was also the first "modern" advocate of Beethoven's piano sonatas. He was, after all, a pupil of Beethoven's pupil Carl Czerny, who had presented him to Beethoven himself in 1823 as Beethoven had been presented to Mozart in 1787. The

Hammerklavier in particular had been "the riddle of the Sphinx," as Berlioz called it, but when Liszt interpreted the work in Paris at the Salle Érard in 1836, Berlioz—who followed with the score in hand—wrote in the *Gazette Musicale:*

> A new Oedipus, Liszt, has solved it. . . . Not a note was left out, not one added . . . no inflection was effaced, no change of tempo permitted. Liszt, in thus making comprehensible a work not yet comprehended, has proved that he is the pianist of the future.

When Liszt was an old man, Wagner (then Liszt's son-in-law) asked him to play the late Beethoven sonatas for him. Liszt's playing of them was still a revelation. (Wagner wanted to hear them privately because he believed they represented "confessions" and ought therefore to remain private.)

Even Brendel acknowledges that Liszt "is the type we aspire to: that of the universal performer of grand stature. To him also we owe our aural imagination and our technique." Brendel's own pianistic recognition of Liszt has extended to both the concert platform and the recording studio. (His credentials as a Lisztian are indebted chiefly to his performances of the Abbé's late music, for elsewhere his performances are respectful and sensible, alas, but not exciting—and old-fashioned excitement is an essential ingredient in much of Liszt's music.) Schnabel, too, regarded Liszt as a superior musician because he was a "*creative* virtuoso; he composed, he conducted, he taught, he wrote, and he kept in contact with some of the best brains of his generation." (Schnabel nonetheless jettisoned Liszt's music from the repertoire he played in his maturity. Although Schnabel's devotion to music that was, as he described it, better than it could be played has been held up as proof of his seriousness, I must admit that such pomposity sounds to me only like an excuse for playing badly. After all, the Liszt sonata and the Schumann *Fantasia* are also better than they can be played.) Yet, for all his manifest genius (and generosity), Liszt's greatness has been conceded by the academy (notwithstanding his sincere appreciation by non-virtuosos) grudgingly, and through the back door, as it were. Indeed, the academy's fondness for Liszt's desolate and startling late music has led to a tolerance, if not to an actual appreciation, of its more glamorous and fantastic antecedents, such as the operatic transcriptions and reminiscences, the *Rhapsodie espagnole* and the Hungarian rhapsodies—the last of which Bartók considered perfect works of art.[5] Rosen:

> The early works are vulgar and great; the late works are admirable and minor. Liszt may be compared to an old ancestor who built up the family fortune by disreputable and shameful transactions in his youth and spent his last years in works of charity; recent criticism reads like an official family biography that glosses over the early life and dwells lovingly on the years of respectability.

These "vulgar and great" works are one of the sources of the contempt that sober, academically minded critics and musicians developed for Liszt and for those who followed him because such music was seen as essentially cheap and the technique required to master it as tarnishing to the dignity of virtuosity—as if, to quote Kaiser again, "even one of those who by their playing are able to set the tone for a decade or more could be reproached with being nothing but a 'pure virtuoso.'" Indeed, Liszt's performances of these early works gave his friend Chopin leave to observe (astutely, if sharply), "when you do not win the public you are able to overwhelm it."

Censure of Liszt's work (and in fact of Liszt as a person) was—and is—not only hateful, but foolish: the *Rhapsodie espagnole* exists alongside the "Bénédiction de Dieu dans la solitude." The simple truth is that Liszt inspired jealousy: genius alone is begrudged, but genius, kindness, beauty, and success together proved intolerable to the common mind and the common soul. Liszt was truly the musical embodiment of the Romantic era: he was a great man, and he was not only receptive to but pioneering in his

---

5. Even Pletnev, Pollini, and Zimerman omit such works from their recorded Liszt recitals (on each of which the sonata is the centerpiece). Pletnev gives the "Dante" sonata, "Gnomenreigen," and "Funérailles"; Pollini, *Nuages gris, Unstern!-Sinistre, La lugubre gondola I* and *R. W.-Venezia;* and Zimerman, *Nuages gris, La notte, La lugubre gondola II,* and "Funérailles."

This generation of pianists is the first not to give Liszt's Hungarian rhapsodies their virtuoso due. As it happens, recordings of them are among the most endearing left to us by virtuosi of the past. (The way Ervin Nyiregyházi played the third, Gilels the ninth, and Novaës the tenth was unforgettable.)

use of new instrumental forms (for example, the programmatic work—of which the instrumental landscape forms an interesting sub-genre), instrumental advancements (the Érard double-escapement action for one, which permitted rapid repetition of a single note), and tremendously broadened conceptions of instrumental virtuosity, such as Paganini's playing revealed to him. The Romanticism of Liszt (as well as Chopin, Berlioz, at one time Schumann, and Wagner) was bitterly opposed by Brahms, Joseph Joachim, Mendelssohn-Bartholdy, and Clara Schumann. In his biography of Chopin (1852), Liszt had defined the opposing schools of Romanticism: his, which "denied that beauty could have an unchanging, absolute form," and the one which "believed in the existence of a form that was permanent, its perception representing absolute beauty." He set forth his and his confrères' credo.

> Not stressing the excellence of form, they sought it only to the extent that its faultless perfection is indispensable to the full revelation of emotion, for they were aware that emotion is maimed as long as an imperfect form, like an opaque veil, intercepts its radiance. And so they subordinated professional craft to poetic inspiration, calling upon patience and genius to rejuvenate the form that would satisfy the demands of inspiration. They reproached their opponents for subjecting inspiration to Procrustean torture, for admitting that certain types of feeling were inexpressible in predetermined forms, and for depriving art in advance of all the works which would have tried to introduce new feelings in new shapes—feelings that come from the ever-progressing development of the human spirit and the instruments and material resources of art.

Ernest Newman defined these opposing schools as "the virtuoso" (Liszt) and "the virtuous" (Brahms). The latter regarded themselves, grandly, as the last bulwarks of morality and tradition in art, and *virtuosi*—both in composition and playing—as corrupters, decadents, immoralists. All of the virtuous were German speakers, while only one of the "virtuosi" happened to be so; Berlioz, Chopin, and Liszt (notwithstanding a period in Weimar) having been French speakers. Thus while Wagner was the composer whose music was heard to best serve the purposes of Nazism, the virtuous contributed to the atmosphere that gave rise to that movement by regarding themselves and the traditions they believed themselves to be upholding as superior to the music created by a Frenchman, a Pole, a Hungarian, and, in the case of Wagner, a native dissident. (Is the fact that so many virtuosi are homosexual another reason that the "virtuous" middle class despised the virtuoso in general? One might even be so bold as to assert that *most* virtuosi are homosexual; that one might more easily say which ones are not homosexual than which ones are.)

The fact that the academy assimilated the virtuous obliged the virtuosi to seek its (and their own) fortunes. The eventual result was the (Lisztian) "Romantic Revival." (Frank Cooper's Romantic Music Festivals at Butler University in Indianapolis between 1968 and 1978, the "Raymond Lewenthal Romantic Revival Series"[6] from the 1970s, Hyperion's "Romantic Piano Concerto" series and the annual "Rarities of Piano Music" festival at Schloss vor Husum, are among its monuments.) At the same time, the "music appreciation" commonplace of (much of) Romantic expression as *ex cathedra* has so conditioned the way we speak and think and write that even non-virtuoso Romantic musical expression is now viewed with suspicion. This is lamentable. Keats, in the sonnet "On Seeing the Elgin Marbles," called the fragments from the Parthenon "a shadow of a magnitude": the academy in our age has become the magnitude, and the creator—the virtuoso above all—the shadow, the modern incarnation of Milton's Lucifer: "but O how fall'n! how / chang'd / From him, who in the happy Realms of Light / Cloth'd with transcendent brightness didst outshine / Myriads though bright."

The individual voice is appreciated ever less. Once upon a fabled time a virtuoso would have withdrawn from the stage if playing would have obliged him to suppress personal and musical identity, for without these there is no greatness. The present condition of the virtuoso transcription—another monument of Lisztian Romanticism, and, in fact, of the whole virtuoso tradi-

6. Elan has reissued some of these recordings: the *Hexaméron*, works by Alkan, concertos by Henselt and Rubinstein, and Lewenthal's arrangement of Busoni's edition of Liszt's *Totentanz*. Lewenthal first performed several of these works at Butler University.

tion—is a commentary on the virtuoso himself: the general absence of it from recital programs confirms that both the form and its avatar (the virtuoso) are no longer held in high esteem. Such an absence also bespeaks an ignorance of the centrality of the transcription to the history of the keyboard: transcription—intabulation, in Italian *intavolatura*—was the first music written for it. What those who nonetheless deny the validity of the transcription—the literalists—will not grant is that the original work is not displaced by it; that, instead of the transcription being the acme of Romantic effrontery and arrogance (as the very Romantic Wanda Landowska, for one, suggested), of frivolity and self-amusement, it is a way of reaching a penetrating understanding of a composer's work.

For *virtuosi* themselves the transcription represents not only an attempt at synthesis and a loving act of creation and criticism in its own right, but a potentially, even often, elevated category of art. The transcriptions of Alkan (the first movement of Beethoven's third piano concerto), Liszt (the "Liebestod" from *Tristan* and Beethoven's third symphony), and Godowsky ("Triana" from Albeniz's *Iberia*), for example, are transcendental things. The transcription allows the virtuoso to play virtually any piece of music ever written: chamber music, lieder, orchestral scores, concerto, opera.[7] The virtuoso's affinity for transcriptions does not, how-

7. The transcription for solo piano of a work originally written for instruments other than piano—or for the piano in combination with other instruments—is the most common exemplar of the art; little-known examples of which include Michel Dalberto's transcription of Strauss's *Vier letzte Lieder* and Mikhail Rudy's transcription of Schumann's *Dichterliebe* (composed as an homage to the pianist whom Rudy most admired in performances of this cycle: Benjamin Britten). Nonetheless, works originally written for the keyboard have themselves often been transcribed: Beethoven sonatas, by Silcher (for voice); the "Largo e mesto" from Beethoven's opus 10, no. 3, for orchestra, by William Hepworth (an organist, composer, and the author of a handbook on string instruments); the *Hammerklavier* sonata by Felix Weingartner, for orchestra; Schumann's *Carnaval,* for orchestra, by—among others—Giampaolo Testoni; Scarlatti sonatas, by Casella (*Scarlattiana*) and Tommasini (*Le donne di buon umore*); five of Rachmaninov's *Études-tableaux,* for orchestra, by Respighi; Chopin mazurkas, by Pauline Viardot (arrangements of twelve for voice and piano). Even the Liszt sonata has been transcribed at least thrice—for fifteen wind instruments (by Janos Komives), for orchestra (by Vladimir Ashkenazy), and for organ (by Bernhard Haas).

ever, preclude in any way an equal command of, or at-homeness in, Beethoven sonatas or Brahms concerti. Zimerman (a champion of both these composers) transcribed J. S. Bach's passacaglia and fugue, BWV 582,[8] and his performance of it remains the most surpassing Bach playing I have ever heard in concert. (I have been fortunate to hear him play it twice: the first time in Perugia on a day which, incidentally, began in Positano with a walk through the garden of one of history's supreme transcribers of Bach's music, Wilhelm Kempff; the second in Florence. The former concert opened with the transcription and the latter one ended with it.)

Virtuosity is less anarchic than extravagant (like Mannerist painting, or the singing of the *castrati*), so it is surprising that piano *virtuosi* should excel in the interpretation of the lapidarian music of the late Baroque and early classical periods (periods abundant in *virtuosi*); that, indeed, the Bach revival should have come in the Romantic era (only partially thanks to the first public performance of—a doctored-up version of—the *St. Matthew Passion*, led by Mendelssohn-Bartholdy, in Berlin, in 1829; Forkel's 1802 biography of the composer having already done much to set

8. Josef Wagner opened a May 1934 recital in Rome with his own transcription of this work. (I am supposing the transcription was Wagner's because no transcriber's name was given in the program, and Wagner happened to be a composer as well as a pianist.) One learns from Sorabji's review of a May 1935 recital in London by American pianist and composer Anton Bilotti that BWV 582 was transcribed for piano not only by Bilotti himself, but also by Fritz Malata (a pianist and composer who was born in Vienna and died—a suicide—in Frankfurt-am-Main.) Three of Zimerman's colleagues have transcribed (and recorded) the work for the piano as well: Emile Naoumoff, Awadagin Pratt, and Igor Zhukov.

An enterprising recording on the Signum label brings together a performance of the passacaglia and fugue in its original form—on a 1769 Silbermann organ (although the work may actually have been written for pedal cembalo)—with transcriptions of it by Eugène d'Albert (piano), Max Reger (four hands on two pianos; the same forces for which Chasins and Gino Tagliapietra made their transcriptions) and Stokowski (orchestra), as well as a Liszt/Johann Gottlob Töpfer arrangement for Romantic organ.

In all, more than thirty transcriptions of the work are extant. If it was actually written for a two-manual pedal cembalo, however, even organ performances are reinstrumentations of a sort—leaving Gunnar Johansen's recording, for which he employed a double-keyboard piano, perhaps the closest thing to Bach's original.

the ball of appreciation rolling) as what Kaiser defined as "the ever impossible attempt to recuperate from one's own discord in the grandeurs and delights of the past." (Although Gould is celebrated above all as a Bach player, he was uniquely responsive to English keyboard music of the sixteenth and seventeenth centuries as well—William Byrd and Orlando Gibbons—as is, now, Grigory Sokolov.)

In short, *virtuosi* do not look at the repertoire as an either-or proposition, since genius is necessarily promiscuous. It is here that they most radically part company from the academy, where an evident morality is in place. The academy has become the new seat of authority, where self-referential, agenda-driven, occasionally parasitic texts count for more than primary ones, and prosaic performances for more than virtuoso interpretations. Though it confounds the academy, what Wilde wrote of Anton Rubinstein in *The Critic as Artist* (Part Two) must remain the definitive and ideal Romantic virtuoso model:

> When Rubinstein plays to us the *Sonata Appassionata* of Beethoven he gives us not merely Beethoven, but also himself, and so gives us Beethoven absolutely—Beethoven re-interpreted through a rich artistic nature, and made vivid and wonderful to us by a new and intense personality.

Perhaps it is obvious; yet I should not want for virtuosity to be misunderstood as anything other than a marriage of interpretive and technical superiority. For the virtuoso, there are no (or at least very few) technical impediments to the realization of an idea; understanding, of course, that while technical perfection is nothing in and of itself (when Mozart and Clementi "dueled" at the keyboard, the former judged the latter to be only a "*mecanicus*"[9]), artists who are mastered by the physical properties of their art (rather than masters of them) are excluded from its highest ranks. Georges Duhamel described the virtuoso as "notre

---

9. Mozart's testimony must be taken with a grain of salt, for he was often nasty in his assessments of other players. Beethoven, who had no axe to grind with Mozart, described his playing to Czerny as "neat and clean, but rather empty, flat and antiquated." In any case, Clementi—and not Mozart—made the greater contribution to virtuoso piano playing.

représentant, celui qui dit ce que nous ne savons pas dire," then explained, "Quand je célèbre un virtuose, j'exalte mon grand amour personnel de la perfection."[10]

Among all *virtuosi*, Cortot had the most elusive technique, yet even on his spastic days his playing was described as "the playing of a god," his wrong notes regarded as "the wrong notes of a god." Apologies for Cortot's faults—apologies he himself did not beg—demean what was great about his virtuoso playing. His 1933 recording of Chopin's F minor ballade, for example, is a supreme performance. (In addition to being a virtuoso, Cortot also taught, wrote, edited, and conducted—most notably, in 1902, the Paris première of Wagner's *Götterdämmerung*.)

Occasional fallibility does not detract from the glory of virtuoso playing—Serkin, for one, could be off one day and staggering the next—yet most people find listening to a pianist whose performances are marked by chronic technical instability at best unrewarding and at worst nerve-wracking because they make it impossible to trust and surrender to him. The performance of a reliable pianist may be yet more disappointing, however: without the possibility of the transcendent experience, music is sad.

As it is, I once planned to teach in the academy. I pursued a doctorate in modern British literature for three years, and prepared to write a dissertation on music in the novels of Forster. The idea, however, was spoiled for me by the academy itself (literature, fortunately, was not) because there theory is a demi-god and the new Trinity—initially liberating, now Procrustean—is race, class, and gender.

I decided, then, that I would not allow the same fate to befall my experience of music. (Inevitably I write on some of the subjects that have attracted the untoward attentions of theorists, but without, I pray, an ideological impulse—only an aesthetic one.) Indeed, in music I prefer to be *un amateur*, in the French sense, to anything else. From 1982 I was a familiar—if not a friend—of Horowitz. Like so many before me, I made the pilgrimage to the

---

10. "[O]ur representative, the one who says that which we are incapable of saying," then explained, "When I celebrate a virtuoso, I exalt my own great love of perfection."

townhouse on Manhattan's East Ninety-Fourth Street to listen and to learn.

In retrospect, Horowitz is (or was) to the twentieth century as Liszt was to the nineteenth; the very incarnation of the piano, the one whose name alone denotes the zenith of virtuoso art. And as with Liszt, critical opinion of Horowitz ranged from the most extravagant praise to the most severe condemnation. James Hilton wrote (in addition to the novels *Lost Horizon* and *Good-Bye, Mr. Chips*) that "if by some dispensation a man born deaf were to be given hearing for a single hour, he might well spend the whole time with Horowitz," while Neville Cardus, after hearing Horowitz play at Queen's Hall, London, in May 1931, gushed, "I am ready to believe he is the greatest pianist alive or dead." Michael Steinberg, on the other hand, concluded his entry on Horowitz for *The New Grove*, "Horowitz illustrates that an astounding instrumental gift carries no guarantee about musical understanding." (Steinberg, not surprisingly, pitches his tent in the Brendel camp.)

The most famous negative article in the Horowitz literature, Virgil Thomson's "Master of Distortion and Exaggeration" from the *New York Herald Tribune* (7 March 1942), offers, on its surface, a neat *resumé* of the complaints leveled against the contemporary virtuoso—even as Thomson's reviews of concerts by other virtuosi (Hofmann, Landowska, Josef Lhévinne, and Arthur Rubinstein, among others) during the same period (and for the same newspaper) demonstrate that he was not, *a priori*, antagonistic to virtuosity at all.

> If one had never heard before the works Mr. Horowitz played last night in Carnegie Hall, or known others by the same authors, one might easily have been convinced that Sebastian Bach was a musician of the Leopold Stokowski type, that Brahms was a sort of flippant Gershwin who had worked in a high-class night club and that Chopin was a gypsy violinist. One might very well conclude also that Liszt's greatest musical pleasure was to write vehicles for just such pianists as Vladimir Horowitz. The last supposition would be correct. Liszt was that kind of pianist himself, and he turned off concert paraphrases of anything and everything from the *Faust* waltz to Palestrina motets. Whether he was quite the master of musical distortion that Horowitz is, history does not record; but I think there is

little doubt possible that a kinship of spirit exists between the two pianists. One has only to hear Horowitz play Liszt's music to recognize that.

Do not think, please, that my use of the word *distortion* implies that Mr. Horowitz's interpretations are wholly false and reprehensible. Sometimes they are and sometimes they are not. His Bach is no worse and no better than Stokowski's, on which I take it to be modeled. . . . His Chopin varied a good deal during the evening. The sonata was violent, coarsely conceived, melodramatic. . . .

Supernormal would be a better word for the way he renders the works of [Liszt]. He seems to have a perfectly clear understanding of what they are about and a thorough respect for them. He exaggerates when exaggeration is of the essence, but he never tampers with their linear continuity. He makes all the right effects, and he makes them in the right places. The only distortion is one of aggrandizement. He plays the Liszt pieces faster and louder and more accurately than anybody else ever plays them. Sometimes he plays the music of other composers that way too, and the effect is more tremendous than pleasant. In Liszt it is both tremendous and pleasant, because Liszt's music was written for that kind of playing and because Mr. Horowitz really loves and understands that kind of music. It is the only kind that he approaches without fidgeting, and last night it was the only kind the audience didn't cough through. If I speak chiefly of interpretation, it is not that I am wanting in admiration of Mr. Horowitz's justly acclaimed technical powers. But these powers are exploited by a violent and powerful personality that is, after all, a part of his virtuoso equipment. . . . And almost any of the more poetic virtuosos . . . has a lovelier tone. But none of these pianists is so free from respect for the composer's intentions, as these are currently understood. Horowitz pays no attention to such academic considerations. He is out to wow the public, and wow it he does. He makes a false accent or phrasing anywhere he thinks it will attract attention, and every brilliant or rapid passage is executed with a huge crescendo or with a die-away effect. It is all rather fun and interesting to students of what I like to call the wowing technique.

An extraordinary piece of writing, as well as an untruthful one! The Bach pieces (two chorale preludes and the C major toccata) were Busoni transcriptions and therefore not modeled on Stokowski's Bach at all. (Stokowski's may have been modeled on

Busoni's, however.) The characterization of Liszt and his music is a cartoon. Also, as is even now fashionable in the circle with which Thomson allied himself, Liszt's virtuoso achievements are misrepresented. Berlioz's testimony to Liszt's faultless interpretation of Beethoven's *Hammerklavier*, like the written reactions of Chopin and Ignaz Moscheles to Liszt's playing of their music, refutes any idea that he was "a master of musical distortion"—unless he chose to be, and that is an altogether different matter. And as for Chopin's B-flat minor sonata, it *is* violent. Schumann wrote of it: " . . . one must confess that from this songless and cheerless movement [the finale] there breathes a special and dreadful spirit, suppressing with resolute fist every inclination to resist."

When, in the first paragraph, Thomson identifies Liszt as "that kind" of pianist and then, in the third, claims that Liszt's music was written for "that kind" of playing and that Horowitz "really loves and understands that kind of music," one wonders for a moment what, precisely, he means by "that kind." "Distortion" and "exaggeration," as well as "melodramatic," "affected," "personality" and "normal" (tucked into a subordinate clause at the end of the second paragraph) erase any uncertainty, and also intensify the collaborationist or informant tone of the review. Horowitz was both Jewish and homosexual (the latter an open secret even then), so Thomson's portrayal of him and his playing as abnormal in 1942—knowing the treatment of Jews and homosexuals in Europe at that moment, and considering that he himself was homosexual (even as he pretended to heterosexuality[11])—tells much more about himself than about his subject.

Thomson's is, most emphatically, far more than a composer's anxiety over an interpreter's prerogative. I decline to make a moral judgment about his closetedness because I understand that the social context of the 1940s made him—and many like him—believe in its necessity. Horowitz was guilty of the same

11. Thomson represented the writer Mary Butts, with whom he was friendly for half a century, as the love of his life—a representation that his biographer, Anthony Tommasini, rebuts. Although she married twice (her second husband was the homosexual painter Gabriel Atkin), Butts was no stranger to Sapphism.

cowardice—at least publicly. Yet I must condemn Thomson's making a personal moral judgment of Horowitz in a public forum: music was the occasion for the article, but not its real subject. Thomson's piece is a superb illustration of the ways representations of the virtuoso have been—and may still be—deformed for extra-musical motives. This is a theme to which I shall return.

Though he himself disliked the appellation, Horowitz was sometimes called "The Last Romantic"; meaning the same thing, he called himself "the last of the Mohicans." Still, he wrote in his own notes to *Horowitz at Home:*

> A dictionary definition of 'romantic' usually includes the following: 'Displaying or expressing love or strong affection; ardent, passionate, fervent.' I cannot name a single great composer of any period who did not possess these qualities. Isn't, then, *all* music romantic?

The answer, of course, is that only for the Romantics is all music Romantic, all music virtuoso; even if only by virtue of the fact that music is the highest—because the most expressive—of the arts.

2.

"Le concert, c'est moi."

—*Franz Liszt, Letter to Cristina Trivulzio
principessa di Belgioioso*

The virtuoso, approaching every interpretation as a unique occasion, is generally willing to dare, to risk, to go all out. Pollini, to give but one example, takes magnificent chances in concert; so did Arrau (as his live recordings of the Liszt sonata prove). Even a virtuoso interpretation that flops can compel as a document of imagination and courage. A less flawed non-virtuoso rendition, by contrast, can be merely one more interpretation-in-progress, a whistle stop on the way to one theoretically ideal interpretation—as if an objectively perfect interpretation (or any objective interpretation) could exist or be desirable. This is precisely what Liszt argued against, and quite rightly. Indeed, any worthwhile composition calls for multiple views of itself in the same way that all of Piranesi's Roman views and *capricci,* or Monet's series of paintings of the cathedral at Rouen, suggest the totality of those glorious places; in the same way that all of the great actors who have taken the role of Hamlet have—collectively more than individually—shown the complexity of Shakespeare's man.

The virtuoso interpretation expresses more potentialities than any other, without, however, aspiring to be the last word. Horowitz professed never to play a work the same way twice; Sofronitsky, too, chose from many possible interpretations in the moment. By contrast, Brendel's constant revisiting of the Beethoven sonatas and concerti suggests very strongly that a final statement is *his* grail, just as it was Schnabel's. Put another way: Horowitz admires the rare butterfly in the meadow and walks on; Brendel wants to capture the butterfly in his net, then mount it under glass with its beautiful wings pinned open. The passion of the latter is the passion of the collector, the work of art being for him, in the end, a trophy testifying to his acumen. I cannot but wonder whether the desire to pin down this one perfect performance actually derives from an impulse to claim the composer's very identity, almost to become the composer at the moment of that one perfect performance. If this is so, then the virtuoso is, in fact, the more modest interpreter.

The highest accepted general virtues for a musician are, at present, sacerdotal: a unity, as well as a steadiness, of spiritual, moral, and intellectual qualities, allied with a sense of "service." But *virtuosi* often remain apart from formalized religion because humor and irony and eroticism—conspicuously absent from mainstream religious discourse—are indispensable in music. Liszt, who late in his life took minor orders of priesthood, was the perfect and literal synthesis of the sacerdotal and the free, even pagan. (When we speak of placing composers and performers in a "pantheon," we are expressly and potently affirming the pagan: a pantheistic order is explicit in the word.)

Romain Rolland described virtuosity in volume 4 of *Jean-Christophe* (a *roman-fleuve* about a composer) as "a physical pleasure, the pleasure of skill, of agility, of satisfied muscular activity, the pleasure of conquering, of dazzling, of enthralling in his own person the many-headed audience: an excusable pleasure, in a young man, almost an innocent pleasure, though none the less destructive of art and soul." (I am afraid that I regard pleasure as the life-blood of both art and the soul. Indeed, I cannot conceive of pleasure as an object of moral censure; nor, I know, can the virtuoso.) With the advent of the public concert, a kind of rampant high-octane playing developed—one brought to its peak, in this century, by Simon Barere, György Cziffra, Marc-André Hamelin, Arcadi Volodos,[1] and Earl Wild—yet possession of supreme tech-

---

1. Volodos is in the miserable position of playing (or having to play) highly virtuosic works—among them some of Horowitz's own *spécialités de la maison*—

nical mastery is essential to performances of virtuoso music that
is not generally denominated as virtuosic in the derisive sense:
Albeniz's *Iberia,* Boulez's second sonata, Brahms's *Paganini* variations, Busoni's *Fantasia Contrappuntistica,* Chopin's F minor Fantasie, the Liszt sonata or (Busoni's arrangement of the) fantasy on
"Ad nos, ad salutarem undam" (from Meyerbeer's *Le Prophète*),
Mendelssohn-Bartholdy's *Scherzo a capriccio* in F-sharp minor,
Gaspard de la nuit, Schubert's *Wanderer* fantasy, and *Kreisleriana.* It
is no less essential to performances of music by three composers
(Debussy, Sorabji, and Stravinsky) who wrote essays against the
virtuoso yet made cruel demands of him (the Frenchman in his
études, the Englishman in his *Opus clavicembalisticum* and the
Russo-Gallo-American in his *Trois Mouvements de Pétrouchka*[2]).
Stravinsky, like Rolland, had little love for "go-getting and tyran-
nical *virtuosi,*" yet realized that "verbal dialectic is powerless to
define musical dialectic in its totality" and so placed one principal condition on the interpreter: "that he be first of all a flawless
executant."

Stravinsky defined perfection in an interpreter as "con-
sciousness of the law imposed on him by the work he is performing." Among the most striking examples of Stravinskian
perfection is Ivo Pogorelich's recording of Brahms's intermezzo
opus 118, no. 2. At 8'49", it is nearly twice as long as Kempff's
(4'28" for Decca, and 4'32" for Deutsche Grammophon). Yet
is one pianist more conscious than the other of the "law" of
the score? To my mind, no. Though Pogorelich has the superior
mechanism (concert performances of *Gaspard de la nuit,* Schumann's *Symphonic Études,* and *Islamey* stunned me), both his and
Kempff's intermezzi are lawful: while Brahms's tempo marking
of *Andante teneramente* theoretically sets parameters for interpre-

---

in order to gain attention, and unsensational works in order to gain the approba-
tion of (conservative) critics. The booklet note for his Carnegie Hall recital début
recording was written by Harris Goldsmith, a self-avowed nonworshiper of "py-
rotechnical acrobatics," and I cannot but wonder whether he was engaged for the
task so as to legitimize this pianist (who, possibly, deserves better). That Schumann's *Bunte Blätter* was, for Goldsmith, the high point of Volodos's recital deep-
ens this impression.

2. As difficult as Stravinsky's *Pétrouchka* movements are, Gilels made them
yet more difficult and more pianistic in his version of them.

tation of the intermezzo, it is an imprecise indication; it is not like the 90 degrees in a right angle or the boiling point of water on the Celsius scale. (Indeed, Brahms has been called "the first Impressionist.") Only a virtuoso of the highest order can play the way Pogorelich does. His unorthodox interpretations have led critics to call him a mountebank or a musical snake-oil salesman, but I am persuaded that he is a truly great pianist. Although Rubinstein's 1953 recording of this intermezzo, at 5'04", is closest to *my* ideal conception of the piece, these three interpretations, taken together, demonstrate the uniqueness (worthy of celebration) of every virtuoso and every virtuoso performance.[3]

Listening to these performances reminds me of Eliot's observation in *Middlemarch* that "time, like money, is measured by our needs." That each generation plays more slowly than the one before it, particularly since the Second World War, is almost a law; as if "the past" can fill the emptiness at the heart of human experience, the booming absence that Forster discovered in the Marabar Caves. Thus Bernstein, collaborating with Gould on the Brahms D minor concerto, disagreed so strenuously with the pianist's slow tempi that he actually expressed his objections to the audience before the performance (6 April 1962). Although, at slightly more than fifty-three minutes, their Brahms D minor was extremely long for the day, a decade later Gilels's recording of the same concerto with Jochum and the Berlin Philharmonic took almost fifty-two minutes. Fleisher's recent performance of the concerto with Giulini, in Paris, took about fifty minutes—some six minutes more than his recording with Szell and the Cleveland Orchestra.

The Liszt sonata, too, has become a longer work than it was three-quarters of a century ago. Cortot's and Horowitz's recordings of the sonata—from 1929 and 1932 respectively—take a little less and a little more than twenty-six minutes. Richter (1961) takes about twenty-nine and a half minutes while Arrau (1970) takes a bit more than thirty-two minutes. By contrast, the in-

---

3. Another case of radically different timings is to be heard on the recordings of Haydn's F minor variations by Pletnev and Demidenko: the former takes 8'04", the latter 16'26". Each interpretation is legitimate, although Pletnev's is more in line with the tempos of Haydn's time.

terpretations of Pogorelich (1992) and Pletnev (1998) approach thirty-five minutes.

Several years ago, I heard Harold Schonberg give a lecture on Romantic piano playing. By playing recordings of the same Chopin nocturne by several generations of pianists, he proved that pianists do play ever more slowly—even those who have inherited the Romantic tradition.

The Purity that Corrupts

In *The World of the Virtuoso*, Marc Pincherle writes:

> In condemning virtuosity lock, stock, and barrel, without appeal or nuances, it seems as if one were obeying mainly the tyrannical mania to draw up a hierarchy. On the top level one puts the musical idea, the "pure" idea, separated from its material, "a reflection of the great unconscious universe," and far below it the realization of that idea—the instrument, the instrumentalist, technical skill, virtuosity.

Pincherle himself, far from putting the virtuoso below the "idea," asserts that without the virtuoso we would not know that musical masterpieces exist. (This is also the gist of Paul Valéry's "Esquisse d'un éloge de la virtuosité." The poet describes the virtuoso as "the one who, par excellence, gives life and reality to what was only writing. . . .")

The validity and aesthetic utility of historical performance (or, in more recent parlance, "historically informed" performance) as an approach to music making cannot be disputed so long as "authentic" instruments and "authentic" performances are not looked upon as *de rigueur*; so long as the sounds produced by original instruments are not put forward as the ideal to which a composer such as Beethoven aspired. (Beethoven, in fact, constantly exhorted piano manufacturers to improve the piano because the disparity between the instrument's capability and his requirements for it was too great. Witness his persistent problems with broken hammers and strings.) To be sure, the most persuasive interpretations of the music of previous centuries take into consideration the inescapable fact that our ears have heard— or have inherited the sounds of—the automobile, the television, two world wars, the atomic bomb. Walter Benjamin argued that the history that a work of art has experienced is part of the essence of its authenticity.

Instrumentalists have been known to assume a rather haughty tone about their historical authority. Although Bach left the *tempi* and the dynamics of the forty-eight preludes and fugues of the *Well-Tempered Clavier* to the taste and training of the performer, Landowska once said to Tureck, "You play Bach your way and I'll play him *his* way." Landowska's performances were one proof that the composer's way really meant *her* way—that is, fidelity to the spirit instead of to the letter; her souped-up Pleyel instrument, another proof.[4]

The historical performance movement has taken on the role of musical super-ego, intent on providing a corrective for a culture dissipated, in its view, by what to others is adaptability. Certainly it has its evangelical aspects. Yet the paring down of scores and musical forces—an implicit rebuke of the dominant musical culture—often gives rise to joyless music making. Thus the acclaimed Beethoven concerto cycle of Robert Levin, John Eliot Gardiner and the Orchestre Romantique et Révolutionnaire must be accounted a pyrric victory for historical performance: the performances testify to scholarship and help satisfy our curiosity, but the sound is ugly and Levin's playing more intrusive than impressive. (Give me Hofmann with Barbirolli in this concerto, or Arrau with Colin Davis!)

As cultural ideas of human beauty change, so do conceptions of artistic beauty: the Ur-piano, if it exists, must be the one that produces the sound to which a particular age is the most accustomed, not the one with the longest history.

Heinrich Neuhaus, the teacher of Gilels and Richter, believed there were essentially four different performing styles: the style devoid of style, the "mortuary" style, the "museum" style, and one to which he gave no name but which is obviously the "virtuoso" style (one "illumined by the penetrating rays of intuition

---

4. Landowska, in a piece titled "Authenticity in the Interpretation of Music of the Past," wrote, "With the Jesuits I say, 'The result sanctifies the means' . . . . little do I care if, to attain the proper effect, I use means that were not exactly those available to Bach."

and inspiration; a contemporary, vivid performance, backed by unostentatious erudition, imbued with love for the composer that prompts the wealth and diversity of technical methods"). Although the word "museum," when used as an adjective, is generally intended to signify lifelessness, Neuhaus considered the museum style and the mortuary style to be completely dissimilar. He illustrated the former, which he regarded as valuable and vital (and possibly also visual), with the example of Landowska and the Stross Ensemble playing Bach's *Brandenburg* concerti. He characterized the latter, "mistakenly referred to as the 'cerebral' style," more generally as one in which the performer is so inflexible and pedantic that "nothing is left of [the composer] except a smell of death." Any number of harpsichordists play baroque keyboard music with more *éclat* than any number of pianists, yet with earlier instruments the dialogue between epochs is sometimes lost, precisely because the *matière de son* "dates." What Gilels, for example, did with Couperin and Rameau on the piano has a unique vitality—and, in consequence, musical authority.

Two spokesmen for performances of Chopin's music on instruments from the composer's day are Cyril Huvé and Emanuel Ax. Huvé has recorded the first two of the ballades and scherzi on a Pleyel (Chopin's preferred make) from 1828/1829, and the second two of each on an Érard from 1838. In his own notes for the recording, Huvé, who studied philosophy as well as music, deflects attention from his own playing to the instrument itself in order "to advance the idea of an 'Ur-piano' and to suggest that it makes possible a more vigilant interpretation of the Urtext." Further, "such pianos force upon us a more exploratory style of playing and less comfortable listening, an understanding of Chopin as more classical in his composition, but more violent in his expression."

Huvé's cheerleading for these instruments, on the evidence of his playing, appears to be a red herring; a disingenuous or self-deluding attempt to conceal his own limitations in Chopin's music. (We would have had to have heard Horowitz and Michelangeli play an Érard or a Pleyel. Neither of these pianists ever elected to play an earlier incarnation of the piano, however—at least not in public.) Indeed, Huvé proves the exact opposite of the phrase "It is a poor workman that blames his tools." After all, not even one of the most illustrious Chopinists (excepting those who lived during the nineteenth century) has depended on a nineteenth-century instrument. His contention that "musicians prefer the relatively neutral tone of modern instruments" because "it is difficult to find an original piano dating back to the Romantic era in a condition which meets the artistic demands of the pieces concerned" does little to advance his argument. Finding a piano dating from the Romantic era is beside the point; finding a pianist who understands the period and has the resources to bring that understanding to fruition is not. As Cardus so lyrically put it in his mid-century essay "Chopin and Pianists," "Chopin was romantic and aristocratic, and where to-day is romance or aristocracy?"

For Huvé's subsequent Adés recording, of Liszt's 1838 "melodic studies," he uses a modern Steinway. His later recording of Liszt's *Album d'un voyageur* (first version of works finally published in the *Années de Pèlerinage*) was made on a piano from about 1835. This to-ing and fro-ing on the matter of instruments suggests that Huvé the Philosopher may well be Huvé the Pianist's worst enemy. (As it happens, Jean-Yves Thibaudet—one of Huvé's countrymen—showed himself to know something about romance and aristocracy when he recorded a Chopin disc using both a modern piano and the Broadwood upon which the composer himself performed when, in 1848, he visited England. His handling of the earlier instrument is as natural and authoritative as Huvé's is self-conscious and unpersuasive.)

In the end, any musician who places himself behind the Urtext, behind the Ur-piano, behind history, behind "purity," behind "the composer's intentions"[5]—one, in other words, whose pathologically reverential attitude toward classic masterpieces

---

5. Most pianists play the *Préludes* of Chopin as a set, although, as Jeffrey Kallberg indicates, this was not the composer's plan for them at all. They were to be preludes to other works—an impromptu, for instance. When played as a set, each prelude save the last is a prelude to a prelude. Ignace Tiegerman did not play them as a set: he gave the A-flat prelude, then the A-flat ballade, for example. Pachmann, too, played individual preludes. His Rome recital of 27 March 1926, for instance, featured a Chopin group made up of the first opus 27 nocturne, the mazurka opus 24, no. 4, the prelude no. 19, the *Polonaise-Fantasie* and the fourth

"does not make them a stimulus instead of an oppression" (Tovey)—fails the composer as well as himself. The Austrian critic Eduard Hanslick, reviewing Brahms's own piano playing (1862), made this astute point:

> It may appear praiseworthy to Brahms that he plays more like a composer than a virtuoso, but such praise is not altogether unqualified. Prompted by the desire to let the composer speak for himself, he neglects—especially in the playing of his own pieces—much that the player should rightly do for the composer. His playing resembles the austere Cordelia, who concealed her finest feelings rather than betray them to the people.

—a criticism that bears in part on Huvé's playing as well, for though he addresses himself to many Urs, he omits the most important: what Lipatti called the Ur-spirit. Ax, for his part, recorded the second concerto, *Grand Fantasia on Polish Airs,* and *Andante spianato and Grande Polonaise* on an Érard (from 1851). Ax's results are pretty, but nothing more, because the instrument itself—not Ax's interpretation—seems to be the *raison d'être* of the recording. The music and the instrument are consigned to museum culture—interesting and perhaps informative, but detached from our lives.[6] Ax presents an enormous contrast to a unique—and living—performance of the Chopin nocturnes on an 1836 Pleyel by Michèle Boegner.[7] The fact that the instrument

---

scherzo. Mischa Levitzki not only performed a selection of the preludes, but played some of them twice through.

Christian Zacharias has on a number of occasions played a program of preludes by Debussy and preludes from Bach's *Well-Tempered Clavier*—an illuminating recontextualization.

6. Zimerman's latest approach to the Chopin concerti, which he played with the Polish Festival Orchestra to commemorate the sesquicentennial of the composer's death, is imaginative, presumptuous, thoroughly operatic.

Chopin's orchestrations of his concerti have inspired a considerable amount of discontent among musicians. The E minor concerto has been reorchestrated by Balakirev (who also transcribed the second movement for solo piano), Pletnev and Tausig; the F minor by Cortot.

7. Edmund Battersby, Patrick Cohen and Peter Katin, among others, have used early nineteenth-century instruments for recordings of Chopin's music as well: respectively, a Graf from 1825, an Érard *ca.* 1835, and a Collard and Collard square piano *ca.* 1836.

is allowed to speak for itself—disturbing overtones, noisy pedals and all—enables one to hear the works with new ears. (Alas, the same cannot be said of the piano that the London department store Harrods commissioned from Bösendorfer to celebrate its own sesquicentennial and to commemorate the sesquicentennial of Chopin's death. Called the "Model Frédéric Chopin," this is a modern instrument contained within a nineteenth-century-style figured-satin mahogany case with gold-leaf banding, starting at 45,000 pounds sterling.)

The extent to which the mortuary style may be a crutch for the self-conscious performer—to be candid, often the one whose career has stalled out (or never taken off)—is revealed not only by what instrument he plays, but by what he plays on that instrument. Too often, these performers look at the championing of Urtexts as a kind of personal salvation, clinging to holy writ in a way that would have baffled the "gods."

The Exile from Ur

Ideally an "unedited" transcription of the composer's score, Urtext versions are sometimes an editor's own cautious and principled performance. In notable instances, no single text can be established as Ur—as in the case of Scarlatti, of whose more than 550 sonatas not even one exists in autograph. (Early editions of a composer's work, barring evidence that the publisher intruded, are often the Urest version available.) Chopin, as Kallberg has compellingly shown, presents a richly ambiguous case, for while we have manuscripts, the composer sanctioned different published versions of his scores; significant variants may be found among the editions of his works published in England, France, and Germany, as well as in the presentation copies he made of his works—suggesting that "the composer's intentions" were rather supple, and that his own performances were subject to variation from whatever he had committed to paper. Many other significant composers have made revisions and emendations to texts for specific performers and performance occasions, and these, too, muddle the establishment of an Urtext and frustrate any pianist not wanting to make decisions. In order to give his *Ham-*

merklavier sonata maximum chances of a London performance, for instance, Beethoven was prepared not only to tolerate, but to sanction its desecration. The composer wrote to his friend and pupil Ferdinand Ries (19 April 1819):

> Should the Sonata not be right for London I could send another, or you could leave out the Largo and begin the last movement with the Fugue, or alternatively begin with the first movement, then the Adagio, thirdly the Scherzo, and leave out No. 4 including the Largo and Allegro risoluto, or you could simply take the first movement and the Scherzo—I leave this to you, do as you think best. The Sonata was written in oppressive circumstances, because it is hard to write for the sake of earning my bread; I have now come to this![8]

On a less drastic scale, Liszt wrote a cadenza to "Au bord d'une source" (from the Swiss *Year of Pilgrimage*) for the Italian pianist and composer Giovanni Sgambati many years after the score was published and which, consequently, is never played. Such interpolations signify not only textually, but historically, by attesting to the unique technical affinities of the artist for whom they were brought into being—and to the composers' readiness to retrofit their works.

Fortunately, even when there is a single version from the composer's lifetime—or even a unique autograph with no contradictory version—this in no way absolves the performer of the responsibility of making artistic decisions. In Mozart's concerti,

---

8. Beethoven had a profound ability to separate the process of composition and perfection of his work—for him, a nearly Taoist process—from the public life of that work. Ries himself wrote

> After the engraving [of the sonata] had been completed, and I was daily expecting a letter giving me the date for publication, I received this, but with the extraordinary instruction 'Add these two notes at the beginning of the Adagio (which takes up 9 or 10 engraved pages), as its first bar.' I confess I could not help wondering 'Is my dear old teacher really becoming weak in the head?'—a rumour which had spread several times. To send another two notes for so tremendous a work, which had been revised through and through, and had been completed six months earlier!! My astonishment grew even greater when I discovered the effect of the two notes. Never can such effective, significant notes have been added to an already completed piece, even had the addition been intended when the composition was first begun.

for instance, the pianist was expected to ornament, as well as to play his own cadenzas, since for Mozart—as for Liszt—a pianist had to contribute his own creative energy to the performance. Thus to hear performances of several Mozart concerti that employ *only* the notes that Mozart left can be frankly disappointing—and, paradoxically, contrary to what the composer expected. Horowitz's playing of the slow movement of the A major concerto, K. 488 (the only thing Mozart ever wrote in the key of F-sharp minor), on the other hand, shows how much can be done with Mozart's concerti by a virtuoso. (Overall, the most beautiful concert performance of a Mozart concerto that I have heard was one by Gianluca Cascioli. He played the (in)famous C major, K. 467 with surpassing poise and imagination, and his own cadenzas, the one for the first movement articulating the demonic element of much of Mozart's music.) Mozart's works for solo keyboard may also profit from performances that spurn tradition. Mitsuko Uchida, for example, wrote a new ending to the D minor Fantasy, K. 397 which works from the opening bars but ends in the tonic-major instead of the dominant. The first edition of the work (1804) stops with the A-seventh chord in bar 97, so the editor of Breitkopf and Härtel's complete edition of Mozart's works tacked on the subsequent bars—which have a trivializing effect.

Schumann presents other problems. His final editions, which unfortunately happen to be the ones most commonly played (as well as the basis for Henle's Urtext edition, since they represent the composer's *dernière pensée*), are invariably inferior to—less Romantic than—his originals, and in any case certain performance traditions exist apart from any score. In his memoir *I Really Must Be Practicing*, Gary Graffman writes,

> In the Schumann *Carnaval* it was traditional (in the Russian school of piano playing) to play the section entitled "Chopin" rather quietly the first time and even more softly the second time. Schumann's markings, however, indicate that this section is to be played the first time *forte agitato* with many dynamic changes, thus rendering it in complete contrast with the quietly played repetition.

When Graffman played "Chopin" like this at the Curtis Institute, Isabelle Vengerova, his teacher, was outraged. (Rachmaninov had played it *piano*, but omitted the repeat.)

The complexities of Schumann editions are legion: the pianist who intends to play the *Davidsbündlertänze*, for example, must choose between the first version, composed in white heat, the later, Clara-fied one, or possibly a conflation of the two. (The objective of the later revisions is the normalization of the early works, most probably by sane-itizing and heterosexualizing those things perceived as tainted by insanity and perversity and the excesses of youth—encoded, or merely perceived, in musical eccentricities such as wild changes of dynamics or tempi. Before Clara entered his life, Schumann had developed a romantic attachment to—and lived with—a composer and pianist named Ludwig Schunke [the dedicatee of the toccata, opus 7]. And Peter Ostwald, a Schumann biographer, points out that in 1829, while traveling to Italy, Schumann "had one and possibly several homosexual encounters.")

The Dutch pianist Folke Nauta and Horowitz's pupil Ronald Turini have recorded the G minor sonata, opus 22 with the original fourth movement, the so-called "Presto Passionato" (which Clara found "too difficult") rather than the finale Schumann composed to replace it in 1838. (Arrau's recording includes both finales.) Demidenko, in his recording of the F minor sonata, opus 14 took what he thought best from both the first and last editions of the work. (I have heard Pollini, for one, play the first version of this sonata, which omits both scherzi, in concert.) Cortot, Horowitz, Rachmaninov, and Abbey Simon played "Sphinxes" in their performances of *Carnaval*, although Schumann indicated they were not to be played. When Hofmann played *Kreisleriana* during the 1937/1938 season, he omitted the second intermezzo from section two, and dropped sections three and four in their entirety. In the *Études symphoniques* (1837, revised and retitled *Études en forme de variations* in 1852; dedicated to William Sterndale Bennett, another young man his inseparability from whom exposed Schumann to comment), Arrau, Ashkenazy, Cortot, Kissin, Perahia, Pollini, and Richter incorporate the five variations that Schumann deleted from the 1837 version of the work; variations published by Brahms in 1873. Arrau and Cortot play the variations in the same sequence, but the others interpolate them in arrangements of their own devising. Sofronitsky, for his part, plays four of the five posthumous variations; Géza Anda only two. In the same work, Pogorelich plays from both editions, but does not include any of the posthumously published variations. Horowitz played (and recorded) the *Fantasiestücke* opus 111 and *Nachtstücke* opus 23 (numbers 3 and 4) as a suite.[9] All of these interpretations are instinct with genuine musical intelligence, and merit for their creator's membership in the composer's *League of David*.

In short, the further a performance must travel to reach the origin of the music, the more the artist demonstrates the measure of both his conscience and his genius: his virtuosity. "It seems as though he tells Scarlatti what happened to his music after all those centuries" is the way a Dutch writer described Horowitz's Scarlatti playing. In short, a musical score must be a process if it is to survive.

Proust Wept

The ascendancy of historical performance has been coincident with the decline of the Romantic virtuoso concert, even though the latter is a valid historical model in its own right. This owes not only to the dying off of musicians in the Grand Style, but to some Platonic longing for musical purity with which *virtuosi* were—and are—seen to interfere. Rubinstein's "fascination upon listeners," for instance, was described by Hanslick after the pianist played in Vienna (1884).

> his virtues arise from a source rapidly drying up . . . robust sensuality and love of life. That is an artistic endowment in which one is only too happy to pardon many a defect, because, among the moderns, it is so rare. Our composers and virtuosos have little of that naïve, elemental force which would rather dare than brood and which, in passion, acts impulsively and without thought of the consequences. They are dominated by the intellect, by education, by refined and more or less profound reflection. They tend to diffuse bright light with all sorts of blended colours, to subdue passion, and to indulge in circumlocution. . . . Our culture-weary Europe capitulates willingly to this force, rooted in temperament and race, and permits the 'divine Rubinstein' many a special prerogative. Yes, he plays like

---

9. Horowitz never recorded the Schumann concerto, though he once tantalized his admirers by saying that if he did play it—as there was talk that he might during his "Golden Jubilee" year (1978)—it would cause a revolution.

a god, and we do not take it amiss if, from time to time, he changes, like Jupiter, into a bull.[10]

This beautiful review communicates Rubinstein's magnificence to us. At the same time, Hanslick opposes Rubinstein to *virtuosi* when, in fact, he was considered second only to Liszt as a virtuoso: an avatar of virtuosity. Thus, "virtuosity" is again used to describe qualities which are not really inherent in the word.

What Hanslick's assessment does underline is the fact that Romantics never conceive of a "definitive" interpretation; rather they seek a performance of intense communicative power that is, *at that moment*, "perfect": the world, to them, is an impermanence. They embrace mutability as Shelley articulated it in "On Mutability": "We are as clouds that veil the midnight moon; / How restlessly they speed, and gleam, and quiver, / Streaking the darkness radiantly!—yet soon / Night closes round, and they are lost forever." It is this view of the composition as an organic, changing piece of art—a creation that must, as Margaret Drabble wrote, "weather into identity"—that distinguishes the Romantic virtuoso from all other interpreters. Intensely relevant here is this passage from an interview with Michel Foucault:

> I am not interested in the academic status of what I am doing because my problem is my own transformation. That's the reason also why, when people say, "Well, you thought this a few years ago and now you say something else," my answer is, [*Laughter*] "Well, do you think I have worked like that all those years to say the same thing and not to be changed?" This transformation of one's self by one's own knowledge is, I think, something rather close to the aesthetic experience.[11]

10. In Proust's *Within a Budding Grove*, the narrator's grandmother expresses a similar idea of Rubinstein: "piano-playing," he observes, " . . . she did not like to be too finicking, too polished, having indeed had a special weakness for the discords, the wrong notes of Rubenstein."
11. Liszt (twenty-two years of age at the time) said much the same thing in a letter to Heine, who had reproached him for his "weathervane" character:

> . . . should not this accusation under which you are crushing me—and only me—be borne by our whole generation, if we are to be fair? . . . Are we not all rather wavering between a past we no longer want and a future we do not yet know? You yourself, with your noble mission as poet and thinker, have you always been quite able to discern the beams of your own star?

One May I went down to Rome to hear Argerich play the
Schumann concerto. What I wanted to hear was *her* interpretation of the concerto: she is a wonderful critic of Schumann
(whom she calls *"mon ami intime"*), for her playing speaks to her
own transformation. Alas she canceled, and I felt as if Proserpine
had failed to return from the underworld to Enna, in the spring.
Her capriciousness, indeed her willfulness, is the proper of a pagan goddess.

Not until 4 October 1994—the day before my thirty-third
birthday—did I manage to hear Argerich in the flesh for the first
time. The occasion was a memorial concert for Nicolas Economou, who had died subsequent to an accident the previous December, and the place was Munich's Herkulessaal. There were
many performances, as well as a long *Gedenkrede* by Joachim
Kaiser, during the memorial, but the star was Argerich. She
played Schumann's opus 73 *Fantasiestücke* with Maisky, then
Economou's two-piano arrangement of Tchaikovsky's *Nutcracker
Suite* with Vadim Suchanov. Her Schumann made me long to be
holding on to someone, and her Tchaikovsky was so demonic
that the hair on my forearms stood on end. During the Tchaikovsky she did something violent that made me love her even
more: when her page-turner messed up during "Trepak"—small
wonder, given the speed Argerich and Suchanov were playing—
she struck her and turned to the proper page herself.

Since then, I have had the chance to hear Argerich play six
concerts—three of them chamber music, the other three concertos—and each one touched inward places of the soul. Even more
than the Munich concert, though, the one to which I return in
memory is a sensational Prokofiev third concerto in Rome (given
in place of the Liszt A major she had announced), after which
Argerich played an encore for piano alone: the opening of Schumann's *Kinderszenen*. This is the only time I have heard Argerich
play the piano alone other than on a disc. It was not the fact of her
playing "Von fremden Ländern und Menschen" ("Of Foreign
Lands and Peoples"), however, but her *way* with it—so ineffably
beautiful and feeling—that drew tears.

It is the life of the senses the virtuoso's playing awakens,
revives, in us. Argerich, like Horowitz and Richter, makes me feel
things physically as well as emotionally and intellectually, and

that is how I know that she is a *virtuosa*. Indeed, only the virtuoso's art penetrates our bodies as well as our souls and brains. That is why Proust wept when he saw Vermeer's view of Delft.

3.

The Critic and the Spider

The Critic

One of the most wrong-headed passages in recent music writing appears in Edward Said's *Musical Elaborations.* Because he is read and reviewed by academics who, to invert a line of Pope's, "repair to church not for the music but the doctrine there," Said gets away here with a lot of nonsense. (For what it is worth, he trained as a pianist in Cairo with Ignace Tiegerman, a pupil of both the famed—and much-married—pedagogue Theodor Leschetizsky and Ignace Friedman.[1])

Specifically, Said is antagonized by Pollini's recording of the Chopin *études;* an antagonism complicated by Said's foolish dismissal of Chopin with eight hostile words: "the word *salon* pretty much sums him up. . . ." The passage in question (from "Performance as an Extreme Occasion"):

> In Pollini's performance the power and astonishing assertiveness of the playing . . . immediately establishes the distance between these performances and any amateur attempt to render Chopin's music. Moreover, the grandeur of Pollini's technique, its scale, its dominating display and reach completely dispatch any remnant of Chopin's original intention for the music, which was to afford the pianist, any pianist, an entry into the relative seclusion and reflectiveness of problems of technique.

1. Said remembered Tiegerman in "Cairo Recalled," a piece he wrote for the American magazine *House & Garden* (April 1987). Allan Evans has produced, as well as written the booklet notes for, a CD of recordings that Tiegerman made in Cairo and Italy between 1952 and 1965.

Every pianist attends to technical studies in one way or another for, as Hofmann (who studied with Anton Rubinstein) observed, "The pianist's artistic bank-account upon which he can draw at any moment is his technic. . . . I was drilled unrelentingly in [scales], and . . . have been grateful for this all my life." The greatness of the Chopin *études*, however—like those of such of his contemporaries as Alkan, Liszt and Schumann—lies their synthesis of both technical and aesthetic elements. (Tovey considered them "the only extant great works of art that really owe their character to their being Études.") Moreover, Chopin's *études* are written for the pianist who is already a virtuoso: no less a virtuoso than Arthur Rubinstein was "scared to death" of them—in fact, he recorded virtually everything Chopin wrote *except* the *études*. Horowitz confessed that he could play neither the "Winter Wind" (opus 25, no. 11) nor the first, second or seventh *études* from opus 10. Gieseking, according to his own testimony, at one time spent six hours a day practicing the first opus 10 study. And "even this greatest of Chopinists"—as Chasins wrote of Hofmann—nonetheless "found stumbling blocks among the *études*, especially the A minor, opus 10, no. 2, the studies in thirds, sixths, and octaves, and the prodigious 'Winter Wind.'" Paolo Petazzi's notes to Pollini's recording of the studies makes this very point: behind their musical content, they are *études* conceived to demonstrate, not to develop, technique.

Said's perhaps willful misapprehension of the nature of the virtuoso *étude*—extending from Scarlatti's *Essercizi* and J. S. Bach's keyboard exercises, through the studies of Clementi and Cramer and Czerny, Hummel and Moscheles, to the *études* of Bartók, Busoni, Debussy (who dedicated his to Chopin), Godowsky (who made 53 transcriptions of Chopin's studies), Kurtág, Liapunov, Ligeti, Messiaen, George Perle, Rachmaninov,[2] Scriabin, Stravinsky and Szymanowski, as well as to works such as Milton Babbitt's *Partitions, Playing for Time* and *My Complements to Roger* [Sessions]—is an example of his scorn for *virtuosi*,

2. One of Rachmaninov's recital programs from the 1920s was devoted exclusively to studies: Schumann (two from opus 3), Chopin (eight from opp. 10 and 25), five of his own *Études-Tableaux*, Rubinstein (opus 81), Scriabin (two from opus 42) and Liszt ("Waldesrauschen," "Gnomenreigen" and "La Campanella").

as well as of the ease with which theory may diverge from experience. Said, as a piano player, *felt* something when he listened to Pollini's recording of the *études* but declines to describe that inward experience. This is strange, for he is very personal when tracing the set of connections he made upon hearing Brendel play a set of Brahms variations (the ones based on a theme from the B-flat string sextet); variations which he informs us that he himself is able to play.

The fact that Pollini's recording is an astonishing—one might even say Apollinian—achievement is not in question. The problem is that Said writes about it as if it were also an isolated achievement, and it is not. One would say that Said is keenly jealous of Pollini and leave it at that were he not so dismissive of Chopin. Why would he covet Pollini's playing of the *études* (as Chopin coveted the way that Liszt—the dedicatee of opus 10— played them) when he considers their composer nothing more than an "effeminate salon decoration"? Pollini may play the *études* in a manner that gives life to Chopin's dictum that "[the impression of] simplicity is the final achievement," but surely it is mean and short-sighted to single out, and to fault, any pianist for an interpretation that superbly fulfills the inherent requirement of the work. Rosen affirms that the *études* are "no more teaching pieces than Blake's *Songs of Innocence* are poems for small children," while Dieter Hildebrandt observes that Chopin used the study when he "set out to conquer the salons, overpowering princes, diplomats and cardinals, subjugating nobility and money and politics and beauty. . . . He expected them, in other words, to listen to lessons—rather like Brecht."

I have heard Pollini play each season for several years now; all-Beethoven recitals in Florence and Pesaro, installments of his Beethoven sonata cycles, a Beethoven fifth concerto at La Scala, a recital of music by Schoenberg, Schumann and Stockhausen in Rome. The period 1994 to 1997, when Pollini played Beethoven sonata cycles in Berlin, London, Milan, Munich, New York, Paris and Vienna, was one in which his performances were frequently marked by an uncharacteristic brutality. The 1998 Schoenberg, Schumann and Stockhausen recital, however, contained all that was best in the young Pollini—eloquence, power, tonal and architectural beauty. At the same time, his playing seemed more personal than ever before: mad, sincere, humorous, devastatingly tender, perverse. Pollini can be a real sorcerer.

The first time I heard Pollini in concert (New York, 1993) he played a program of Chopin, Boulez and Liszt. His third encore was Chopin's sublime (in the Romantic sense) "Winter Wind" study. (Another Chopin study and Debussy's "Pour les arpèges composés" preceded it.) Said would have us believe that Pollini's playing—possibly even more magisterial a full twenty years after he recorded the studies—alienated each one of us who attended that concert. (Pollini is not a cozy pianist, but we do not seek coziness from his playing: as a musician, he is a Piranesi or a da Vinci rather than a Mary Cassatt or a Caillebotte.) Said fails to enter into the spirit of wonderment that the musician may (and that Pollini does) create for us.[3]

In short, I would rather that Said had written about Pollini's musical personality than about his technique (which is not open to a Marxist interpretation), for that is, I suspect, the real locus of his anxieties. Said claims that "actually *playing* the music is what gives one the most satisfaction and pleasure." Does this mean that Pollini's playing interferes with his own (amateur) pleasure in playing? (To be sure, it is the coolness, not the perfection, of technique that separates him from Egorov.) Pollini the man may be part of the *bourgeoisie*, but Pollini the technician assuredly is not: that aspect of his gift belongs to an aristocracy, a class whose parameters are subtly and disturbingly free. (It puts me in mind of a passage in one of Lenin's letters to Gorki, apropos Beethoven's *Appassionata*: "I want to say amiable stupidities and stroke the heads of people who can create such beauty in a filthy hell.") Said's defensiveness may be predicated upon fear of, even panic over, what Pollini does to him; certainly it is out of proportion.

---

3. Another critic, Allan Kozinn, takes on the rapport between the pianist and the listener in *The New York Times* review of Pollini's 2 November 1998 Carnegie Hall recital of works by Schumann (B minor *Allegro* and C major *Fantasia*) and Chopin (nocturnes, opus 27 and second sonata). Kozinn (here taking up the mantle of Kretschmar in Mann's *Doctor Faustus*) concluded that Pollini "set one thinking about the delicate balance between the objective and the subjective in the way we hear music" and that—here he assumes the mantle of Said—"there was a deficit on the subjective side, a distance between Mr. Pollini and the listener that the facts of the performance were not enough to bridge."

The Spider

One of the purest apprehensions of the Chopin *études* that I know is the story of the spider that Paderewski tells in his *Memoirs*[4]:

> One day I was practising in my little room in Vienna. Among the pieces I was then studying, and which I had to play every day as a finger exercise, was a certain study by Chopin, a study in thirds. I was just starting to work—I lit the candles and sat down at the piano. The room was very dark, you know, there were so many tall shrubs growing close to the window. Then, suddenly in the midst of my playing, there came down from the ceiling right on to the piano desk, something like a tiny silver thread. It attracted my attention and I looked a little closer, and then I saw—a spider attached to it. He hung there motionless and appeared to be listening to my playing, and as long as I played that particular study in *thirds,* the little spider remained there perfectly still on his line.
>
> And now comes the interesting thing. After finishing the study in thirds, I went on to another study—in sixths this time, and the moment I began it, the spider turned himself quickly about, and hurried up to the ceiling. Well, it struck me at the moment as very funny, and I was interested and deeply intrigued. I said to myself, 'Now, I must see whether that spider is really musical or not—whether he meant to come down to listen on purpose, or by accident.' So I suddenly stopped my study in *sixths,* and quickly started again the one in *thirds.* Instantly, down came the little spider! He seemed to slide down his line, and this time to the very end, and sat on the piano desk and listened. He did not seem at all frightened, only deeply interested in the music.
>
> He had aroused my interest greatly and I wondered if he would appear the next morning. I was very curious about him—I felt sure I should see him again. Well, he did appear the moment I began my day's work with the thirds. That little thread still hung from the ceiling, and down he came the moment I touched the piano, and this same thing continued all that day, and the next day and for many weeks he came—he was a faithful companion. Whenever I started the study in

4. Saint-Saëns (from "Observations of a Friend of Animals"): "Mention has elsewhere been made of the spider's taste for music. This I have frequently noticed out in the country when playing the piano. Quite against my will I attracted huge spiders whose vicinity was anything but pleasant to me."

thirds, the little spider came quickly to the piano desk and listened. After a time I arrived so far as to be able to see his eyes—so brilliant, like tiny, shining diamonds. He would sit immovable, or hang immovable I should say, during that Chopin Etude, perfectly content and perfectly quiet. But the moment I stopped that particular study, back he went quickly to the ceiling and disappeared. Sometimes, I used to think, quite angrily.

When the vacation time came I confess I felt strangely anxious about the spider. What would become of him, I wondered. 'Shall I find him when I return?' I asked myself. He had become a part of my daily practice, a kind of companion, and I knew I should miss him. When I returned in September, I looked for him everywhere. I looked for the little line, but it no longer hung from the ceiling. I played my study in thirds, again and again I played it, but I could not find my spider friend. The room seemed empty and lonely without him. What had happened to him? Had some careless housemaid crushed out his little life, or had he, lonely and discouraged with the closed piano and silent room, gone elsewhere? I could only hope so. But the days went on, and I never saw my spider friend again.

In the end it is the response of the spider, rather than that of the critic, which signifies, for it is he who is the pianist's "companion."

RED
SIDE

GREATER LONDON COUNCIL
ROYAL FESTIVAL HALL
GENERAL ADMINISTRATOR: MICHAEL KAYE

RECITAL BY
VLADIMIR HOROWITZ
SATURDAY, 22 MAY, 1982
4.30 p.m.

Management: THE ROYAL OPERA HOUSE

GANGWAY 4
SEAT
27*

ROW
P

£50.00
DONATION £50

STALLS
GUEST

AFTER TWO CONCERTS

Manhood

My first great musical dream was to hear Horowitz in person, and thanks to Jack Pfeiffer, his producer at RCA, I managed to get a ticket to his recital in London on 22 May 1982. I got to the Festival Hall well in advance of the concert, at which Prince Charles was to be present, and took my place (Row P, Seat 27)—directly across the aisle from Mrs. Horowitz's—at the first opportunity.

Hearing Horowitz, that particular day, was both elating and desolating; the latter feeling incongruous, unexpected in such an atmosphere of grandeur and glamour. Indeed, although as a little boy I had wanted to be King of England, after the concert I was not even interested in being introduced to Prince Charles. Instead, after seeing Mr. and Mrs. Horowitz off, I began to walk.

For all its flaws, Horowitz's playing had overwhelmed me, and brought me to realize how small was the world I inhabited, and how vague was the one I pursued. (Indeed, the prospect of returning to Florida depressed and terrified me.) I did not want to be Horowitz—although, for a long time, I wanted to be able to play Schumann the way he could—any more than I wanted to be the King of England, but I did want to find seriousness and worth. In short, Horowitz made me impatient to be a man.

Life

When I went to hear Kissin in Bologna, I took the train from Florence. David, an expert on train schedules, figured out that the last relatively fast train between the two cities left about the time a concert of ordinary length would be over. But Kissin played encore after encore—thirteen before the fire department turned off the lights—and I could hardly have left for so prosaic a reason as catching a train. In the end, I caught a later train about 1:00 a.m. that would get in to Florence about 3:30—the train taking an hour and a half longer than usual so that it would not arrive at its terminus (Naples, I seem to recall) too early in the morning.

I stepped into a compartment occupied by two boys in military uniform. They were asleep when I entered, and asleep when I left, but their solid presence was fine company. Though I did not want to be alone after listening to Kissin, I also did not want to talk.

Finally back in Florence, I took a taxi from the train station to our apartment, and found David, like Messalina, wandering up and down Via dei Neri. "What happened?" he cried. "I thought you were dead."

"Oh, no," I answered, "I'm alive."

4.

Notes on Gourmandism

One Saturday afternoon in Florence I heard the Naples-born Aldo Ciccolini acquit himself of an all-French program at the beautiful Teatro della Pergola (where a notable scene in William Dean Howells's 1886 novel *Indian Summer* occurs). He played Ravel's *Valses nobles et sentimentales*, the composer's homage to Schubert, and *Miroirs* in the first part; Chabrier's *Dix pièces pittoresques* after the intermission. Ciccolini's encores kept us in France, too: Debussy's *La plus que lente*, then "Minstrels" from the *Préludes*. (I like Ciccolini's Debussy playing very much.) Whether the program was too much of a good thing or too little, I am unsure. At all events, it was too much: Ravel showed up Chabrier (just as he shows up Chaminade and much of Fauré).

Because Ciccolini's playing that day had no *éclat*, no muscle (qualities so abundant in the "Alborada del gracioso," the fourth of the *Miroirs*, that Lipatti recorded in 1948), I woolgathered, particularly during all that Chabrier. One of the things that occurred to me was this: the principles of virtuoso playing can resemble those of gourmandism set forth in the book I happened to be reading (honestly I was) at the time, Brillat-Savarin's *The Physiology of Taste* (1825). Here Brillat-Savarin defines gourmandism as "[that] which unites careful planning with skilled performance, gustatory zeal with wise discrimination; a precious quality, which might as well be called a virtue, and is at least the source of our purest pleasures." Ciccolini, it must be said, failed to unite these principles, which are six in number:

> Gourmandism is an impassioned, reasoned, and habitual preference for everything which gratifies the organ of taste. [Strik-

ingly relevant to our purposes if we consider taste as an aesthetic rather than sensory faculty.]

Gourmandism is an enemy of excess; indigestion and drunkenness are offences which render the offender liable to be struck off the rolls.

Gourmandism includes *friandise,* which is simply the same preference applied to light, delicate, and insubstantial food, such as preserves and pastry. It is a modification introduced in favour of the ladies and those gentlemen who resemble them. [Ciccolini certainly played his share of *friandise.*]

From whatever point of view gourmandism is considered, it deserves nothing but praise and encouragement.

From the physical point of view, it is the result and proof of the sound and perfect condition of the organs of nourishment.

From the moral point of view, it shows implicit obedience to the demands of the Creator, who, when He ordered us to eat in order to live, gave us the inducement of appetite, the encouragement of savour, and the reward of pleasure.

England has never been known as a country of gourmands. Pleasure, in Albion, is associated with vice (or, at the very least, decadence), which may be why virtuosi excite a peculiar hostility there. England, after all, is the only country where Liszt was received cooly and where, apart from German-speaking countries, the *petit-maître* Mendelssohn was venerated almost as a god. It is also where Brendel, Lupu, and Perahia make their home.

The French take food—and virtuosi—seriously. France is the land of *foie-gras* and Cortot. It is true that French formality has an element of frivolity to it. It is also true that this marriage of formality and frivolity has given us not only *îles flottantes* and *religieuses,* but such peculiarly charming confections as Saint-Saëns's *Wedding Cake* and those pieces of Satie's which are to be played *"avec une ironie contagieuse," "très chrétiennement,"* or *"de manière à obtenir un creux."*

As for German-speaking countries: it is enough to remark that the Germanic toilet has a *stage* for the examination of that which has been digested and evacuated. Eating and music are duties, respectively, to the body and to a once-exalted culture. (The passing of the *pot-de-nuit* was the end of its greatness.)

The Italians love food—and virtuosi—more than any other

people. They are not reproving and suspicious about it, they are not formal and frivolous about it, and they have no sense of duty to it. Consequently, Italy's tradition of native virtuoso pianists is glorious: Busoni, Clementi, Sgambati, and Enrico Toselli ("il Paderewski italiano"); Ernesto Consolo and Pietro Scarpini; Guido Agosti and Sergio Fiorentino; Dino Ciani (killed in an automobile accident when he was but thirty-two), Michelangeli and Pollini (and, possibly, Pollini *fils*); Massimiliano Damerini and Cascioli; Francesco Caramiello (his recordings of the music of Martucci and Sgambati are tremendous) and Gregorio Nardi; Maurizio Baglini; and Francesco Libetta (his recital of Godowsky's studies on Chopin's opus 10 *études* in Milan, in 1994, thrilled the piano world). *"Virtuoso"* does, after all, come to us from the Italian.

5.

The Circus

On Tuesday, 9 June 1840, at two o'clock, in London's Hanover Square Rooms, Liszt gave the first solo piano performance called "recitals"; each individual work on his program—two movements from Beethoven's sixth symphony, his own transcriptions of Schubert's "Ständchen" and "Ave Maria," the *Hexaméron*,[1] a tarantella and his audacious *Grand Galop chromatique*—being a "recital." (He was also the first to give a recital devoted to the works of a single composer.) It was the year before, in Rome, that Liszt first played without supporting artists in performances that he himself called "musical soliloquies." Until this time (as well as for decades afterwards), concerts were often *assemblages;* an orchestra, a singer, an instrumentalist, a chamber ensemble, and possibly even a juggler or similar novelty act. Chopin's first concert in Paris, which was given at Pleyel's salon in January 1832, featured the following works: a Beethoven quintet, a vocal duet, his own E minor piano concerto, a vocal air, a polonaise for six pianos by Kalkbrenner (played by Chopin, Hiller, Kalkbrenner, Mendelssohn-Bartholdy, Osborne, and Sowinski), another vocal air, an oboe solo, and his own variations on "Là ci darem la mano."

That Italy was the country in which the latter concert was given is apposite, since the piano, like the violin, was born there—the "Arpicembalo di Bartolomei Cristofori ... che fà il piano e il forte," as it was described in 1700. Moreover, the first

---

1. A collaborative work based on "Suoni la tromba" from Bellini's *I Puritani* and constructed as follows: introduction and statement of the theme by Liszt; variation by Sigismond Thalberg; variation by Liszt; variation by Johann Peter Pixis; interlude by Liszt; variation by Henri Herz; variation by Czerny; interlude by Liszt; variation by Chopin; interlude and finale by Liszt.

compositions specifically designated for this instrument were the twelve sonatas for "Cimbalo di piano e forte" by Lodovico Giustini published in 1732 in Florence. In the event Liszt's "soliloquies" were his transcription of the overture to Rossini's *William Tell*, his fantasy on Bellini's *I Puritani*, selections from his studies and fragments, and finally, the then-ubiquitous "improvisations on a given theme."[2] (The custom of the pianist sitting with his right profile to the audience—a position that, incidentally, made optimum use of the lid of the instrument to direct sound toward the audience—was originated by Jan Ladislav Dussek, called "Le Beau Dussek," half a century before.) Liszt's innovation, which nonetheless subscribed to the general form of the *assemblage* (that is, an overture, a "vocal" selection, an instrumental work—and a novelty act) prompted his friend Berlioz to write to him: "With a slight modification of the famous *mot* of Louis XIV, you may say with confidence: 'I myself am orchestra, chorus, and conductor. . . . Give me a large room and a grand piano, and I am at once master of a great audience.'"

The virtuoso concert has since been the medium of some of the loftiest artistic expression in Western civilization, even though metaphors of the circus have often been evoked to describe the virtuoso and the virtuoso recital. Few are so noble as Goethe, who believed that "when another person is vastly superior to you there is no remedy but to love him."

Herewith a few *personae* of the pianistic circus; some of them very much at home there, others very much out of place.

The Strong Man

> If you don't lose five pounds and ten drops of
> blood, you haven't played a concert.
>
> —*Arthur Rubinstein*

2. According to Loesser, the first pianist to play a public piano recital—although it was not called a recital—was probably Ignaz Moscheles, in 1837 (in London). The same source records that Johann Christian Bach (called "the London Bach" and "the English Bach"), the youngest son of J. S., played the very first public clavier solo in London history, in 1768 (2 June). According to Eva Badura-Skoda, the Imperial Court Archives in Vienna record public performances on the piano in that city in 1763.

Tzimon Barto (*né* Smith) is the present concert world's contender for the title of strong man. Like the cellist Zara Nelsova (*née* Sara Nelson) and the pianists Olga Samaroff (*née* Lucy Hickenlooper) and Moura Lympany (*née* Mary Johnstone), he has adopted a "heavyweight" name; apparently "the ancient established English equation of performing instrumentalist with foreignness [that] thrust itself with invincible persistence into latter-day America"—as Loesser wrote some years before Smith was born, in Florida—still persists.[3] Lady Henry voices this English equation of performing instrumentalists with exoticism in *The Picture of Dorian Gray:*

> I have simply worshipped pianists—two at a time, sometimes, Harry tells me. I don't know what it is about them. Perhaps it is that they are foreigners. They all are, ain't they? Even those that are born in England become foreigners after a time, don't they? It is so clever of them, and such a compliment to art.

Although Slavic-sounding names are most commonly taken up, Lhévinne's surname is a hyper-Gallicized version of Levine.

Barto/Smith is also a bodybuilder. He has recorded for EMI, and that company, in the June 1994 edition of its *Notes* previewing *The Best of Barto* (drawn from his first four or five recordings, among which were the Chopin *Préludes,* a meretriciously played Liszt recital, a Rachmaninov third, and Schumann's *Kreisleriana*), presents the pianist as follows: "Der Klavierästet Tzimon Barto, der abends Hochvirtuoses von Rachmaninoff, Liszt oder Schumann spielt, hält tagsüber seiner Körper fit—mit Schwerathletik und Body-Building, nach exaktem Trainingsplan."[4]

The implied connection between "physical culture" and musicianship is fatuous; though muscles are a not unimportant part of virtuosity, they mean little if unallied to soul. Perhaps it is enough to observe that Smith resembles a Chippendale's dancer

3. The actual surname of the eponymous heroine of Bernice Rubens's novel *Madame Sousatzka* is Süsskatz: "The change of name [to Sousatzka] doubled the number of her pupils amongst those who sought a foreign caché and gradually her reputation as a teacher grew."
4. "The piano aesthete Tzimon Barto, who in the evening plays Rachmaninov, Liszt and Schumann in the most virtuosic manner, in the daytime keeps his body fit—with heavy exercise and body-building following an exact training plan."

more than he does Rudolf Nureyev, although on one of his latest recordings his gym body is covered up by a dramatic cloak in the manner of one of those dashing, Heathcliffish heroes on the covers of Harlequin Romances. Yet muscles do not equate with musical strength, as Barto's playing illustrates. (To be sure, neither his muscles nor his name have managed to produce artistic heft.)

Anton Rubinstein was a true Strong Man. His seven historical, ultra-virtuoso recitals were of massive length.[5] The second comprised *eight* Beethoven sonatas, while the fourth was devoted exclusively to the music of Schumann: the *Fantasia*, *Kreisleriana*, *Études symphoniques*, F-sharp minor sonata (opus 11), four of the opus 12 *Fantasiestücke*, one of the *Waldszenen* ("Prophet Bird"), the D minor romance, and, finally, *Carnaval*. His sixth was an all-Chopin concert: the *Fantasie*, six of the *Préludes*, four mazurkas, four ballades, two impromptus, three nocturnes, the *Barcarolle*, three waltzes, the first scherzo, the second sonata, the *Berceuse*, and three polonaises.[6] And when Steinway brought Rubinstein to America in 1872 to advertise its pianos, he played 215 concerts in 239 days—and not even one of them on a Sunday.

Bülow played Beethoven's last five sonatas in a single evening, and on 18 January 1872, Beethoven's sonatas opp. 101, 106, 109, and 110, and thirty-three *Diabelli* variations. In 1876, Brahms played the Schumann *Fantasia*, Scarlatti, J. S. Bach's F major toccata (probably a lost transcription by Clara Schumann), his own *Händel* variations, a Schubert *Adagio* and *Allegro*, the Schumann toccata, and Beethoven's opus 109 sonata—among other

5. He omitted wholesale the music of Brahms from these recitals. It remained for Lamond to give a Brahms recital of Rubinsteinian dimensions. In Vienna in February 1886, he played the opus 5 sonata, one rhapsody, 2 ballades, the E-flat minor scherzo, two capricci from opus 76, and both the *Händel* and *Paganini* variations.

6. Lev Pouishnov's first appearances in England were five recitals at Wigmore Hall that pursued the same general line as Rubinstein's historical recitals: the first contained music by J. S. Bach and Beethoven; the second, music of Schumann and Chopin; the third, music of Liszt exclusively; the fourth, music of Rachmaninov and Scriabin; the fifth, music of Glazunov, Liadov, Glinka-Balakirev ("The Lark"), Tchaikovsky, Mussorgsky, Pouishnov, Liapunov, Rachmaninov, and Scriabin. During the 1937-1938 season, Sofronitsky surveyed the piano repertoire in twelve recitals.

works. Sir Charles Hallé acquitted himself of five sonatas in an 1893 recital in London: Beethoven's opus 110, Chopin's opus 58, Weber's opus 39, Liszt's B minor sonata, and Tchaikovsky's opus 37 (a work that rarely appears on concert programs—I have heard it performed in concert only by Pletnev). Hofmann, the most muscular and athletic of all pianists, played 255 different works in twenty-one consecutive concerts in Leningrad in 1912. Horowitz—also in Leningrad—played a total of forty-four big works and sixty-six smaller ones in slightly fewer than a dozen programs during the 1924-25 season. (Oh, to have heard Horowitz play Ravel, or Medtner, in concert!) Benno Moiseiwitsch played a Chopin recital at the Queen's Hall in London that began with the B-flat minor sonata, took in the twenty-four *études* opp. 10 and 25,[7] and ended with the *Barcarolle*, mazurka opus 41, no. 3, nocturne opus 27, no. 2, and waltz in A-flat major, opus 42. Petri played, in London, on 12 October 1934, Busoni's edition of Bach's *Goldberg* variations (this edition excises ten variations as well as all repeats, touches up the writing, and shapes the remaining variations into three movements), Busoni's *Fantasia Contrappuntistica* (a meditation on Bach's *Art of Fugue* lasting three-quarters of an hour), five of Liszt's *Transcendental* studies, and, as an "extra" (that is, encore), Liszt's *Réminiscences de Don Juan*. And, by way of a last but by no means least example, in 1956 Arthur Rubinstein played seventeen concerti in twelve days at Carnegie Hall.

Barto has made his body the temple, the work of art of which his performances are only a function. For these other pianists, by contrast, strength and stamina were emotional as well as physical, and music was the temple.

Concert programs reflect an age's conception of time, as well as its capacity for concentration. Thus, the contemporary taste for shorter programs is less a commentary on the diminished capac-

7. Moiseiwitsch played the *études* in this unique sequence: opus 10, no. 1; opus 25, nos. 4 and 6; opus 10, no. 9; opus 25, nos. 8 and 7; opus 10, no. 10; opus 25, no. 5; opus 10, nos. 4, 11, 6, 7, and 12; opus 10, no. 2; opus 25, nos. 9 and 2; opus 10, no. 8; opus 25, no. 10; opus 10, no. 3; opus 25, nos. 11, 3, and 1; opus 10, no. 5; and opus 25, no. 12. The program booklet for this concert provides a note on each study.

ities of modern performers—though it *may* be such a commentary—than a reflection of the increasingly preoccupied and unfocused nature of modern listeners (and listening). In any case, the ability to play long and controled concerts is a positive signifier of virtuosity because it indicates sound training and suggests a sense of spiritual and technical limitlessness.

Unfortunately, such qualities are not universally regarded as a plus. Michael White, for instance, wrote that "[t]he genius of Kissin isn't comfortable: it threatens . . . with the sheer alien otherness of its uncompromising stature." An "uncompromising stature" may be threatening, but admittedly it is also right on the mark: Kissin's playing is on the scale of the Grand Canyon or the Himalayas or Niagara Falls, which is why it is apposite that in August 1997 he gave a recital in the vast space of the Royal Albert Hall in London. (Contrary to what his publicity agent may think, however, he was *not* the first pianist to give a recital there: Pachmann was, on 10 July 1903.[8]) White's response to Kissin brings to mind Harold Brodkey's story "Innocence," in which he writes of the heroine:

> [S]eeing someone in actuality who had such a high immediate worth meant you had to decide whether such personal distinction had a right to exist or if she belonged to the state and ought to be shadowed in, reduced in scale, made lesser, laughed at.

The Acrobat

Many people went to hear Horowitz during the 1940s and 1950s, in part, because they hoped that he might topple from the high wire when he played one of Liszt's rhapsodies (the second, sixth or fifteenth) or something else spectacular (for example, his transcription of Sousa's "Stars and Stripes Forever"): the ultimate edge was provided by the knowledge that there was no safety net should he fall. Although certain critics have invested heavily in representing it as such, however, this period of Horowitz's career

8. Pachmann's program consisted of Mendelssohn's *Rondo capriccioso*, Schumann's D minor Romance, Liszt's transcription of Rossini's *La Danza*, Weber's *Invitation to the Dance*, Godowsky's study on Chopin's *Grande Valse Brillante*, opus 18, six of Henselt's *Twelve Characteristic Études*, opus 2, and a group of Chopin pieces (unspecified).

was not the true and complete record of his art: he also played, and made marvelous recordings of, Czerny's "La Ricordanza" variations and Mozart's F major sonata, K. 332 at this time. (During the 1920s, he had played Brahms's opus 5 sonata.) What brought him to an emotional breaking point was his accession to a large public's demand that he walk the high wire.

The problem was not that Horowitz did not take pleasure in his own abilities: he did. Nor was it that Horowitz could not give audiences what pianists schooled in the German repertoire gave them (his 1953 Schubert B-flat sonata and most of his Beethoven sonatas—the "Appassionata," for example—are tremendous; so, too, his Haydn sonatas). On the contrary, the problem was that pianists schooled chiefly in the German repertoire could not give audiences what Horowitz did. (Liszt once in a darkened room played the piano so much in the style of Chopin that the assembled thought it was Chopin, until he lit the candles on the piano and said, "You see that Liszt can be Chopin when he likes; but could Chopin be Liszt?")

In short, Horowitz was in an impossible situation: if he played Brahms and Schubert and Beethoven, he was denounced by critics without the imagination of Sorabji[9] for playing out of school, but if he played Liszt he was denounced by the same dull critics for neglecting Beethoven and Schubert and Brahms and praised for the fabulousness of his Liszt. Horowitz was a product of the Russian school, which was, and is, the most sensuously inclined;[10] and there—regardless of what else he played—a pianist was judged above all by how beautifully he played virtuoso mu-

---

9. In an April 1935 review of new recordings by Horowitz, Sorabji wrote that the pianist was "as consummate in the Beethoven [32 variations in C minor] as in the Debussy [an *étude*], in which his tone-colour is a miracle. He is able to produce a tone of completely different quality in the Beethoven from that of the Debussy. Only the highest pianistic artistry is capable of such a feat."

Sorabji admired Horowitz's Brahms playing as well; not only the *Paganini* variations, but two of the "much-mauled" intermezzi. "Instead of the thick suety texture and mock-profundity with which others treat these pieces," he wrote of Horowitz's 1932 performance of the latter, "they were given with a warm, clear glow of tone-colour, a flexible fineness of phrasing, and a subtly poetic feeling that were pure enchantment." As for Horowitz's performance of the B-flat concerto with Toscanini: it sent Sorabji into an ecstacy.

10. Leschetizsky asked three questions of prospective pupils: "Were you a child prodigy? Are you of Slavic descent? Are you a Jew?"

sic. (Horowitz played Liszt's *Don Juan* fantasy so terrifically in his conservatory-leaving recital that he was given a standing ovation by his jurors.[11]) Thomson's review (quoted earlier) articulates Horowitz's dilemma—one from which he believed his only salvation was to "retire"; as, in fact, he did for twelve years beginning in 1953. Liszt once wrote, "Happy . . . he who knows how to break things off before being broken by them." Horowitz's unhappiness was that of the man who breaks things off after being broken by them.

Before Horowitz's long retirement, however, Lipatti heard him in Paris and wrote afterwards, "Nothing is so sad as stylized and intellectualized music where only intuition and great sensitivity are needed. . . . Horowitz will be the most extraordinary pianist of all times the day he is content to accept himself as he is." (This is reminiscent of a passage from Wilde's *De Profundis:* "It is only by realising what I am that I have found comfort of any kind.")

Incidentally, or perhaps not incidentally, Horowitz owned and loved a painting by Picasso, called *Acrobat en Repos*.

On a few occasions the acrobat actually has fallen. Barere, while playing the Grieg concerto with Ormandy and the Philadelphia Orchestra in Carnegie Hall on 2 April 1951, had a heart attack and died on stage. Louis Moreau Gottschalk only *nearly* gave up the ghost while playing his "La Morte," but within a year the incident had been so embroidered that Amy Fay could write "what a romantic way to die!—to fall senseless at his instrument. . . ."

The Juggler

Leon Fleisher, who plays repertoire for the left hand alone since he developed a form of partial paralysis in his right arm during the 1964–1965 season, did a juggling act in a concert he gave in Florence a few years ago to replace an ailing colleague. In his contribution to *Remembering Horowitz*, Fleisher wrote that, "In an

11. His program was colossal: the Bach-Busoni *Toccata, adagio and fugue,* Beethoven's opus 110 sonata, Chopin's F minor *Fantasie,* Schumann's *Symphonic Études,* Rachmaninov's second sonata, Mozart's G major gigue and, only then, the *Don Juan* fantasy.

effort to reproduce his inimitable, searing brilliance of sound, many a young pianist has wound up with a case of tendonitis or worse. . . ." Significantly, Fleisher refrained from telling whether emulation of Horowitz—as isolated and Romantic a figure as Byron's Childe Harold, Senancour's Obermann, and Shelley's Frankenstein (the supreme monument of Gothic architecture)—precipitated his own condition. On the basis of his 1959 recording of the Liszt sonata, however, one must conclude that his paralysis was probably inevitable. The Liszt sonata may well be one of Fleisher's favorite works, but he plays it here as if he detests it. (A famous Italian critic, after listening to this recording with me, suggested that it would have been better for the piano if Fleisher had lost the use of both of his hands.)

In the event, that afternoon in Florence Fleisher played pretty much the same works he had then recently recorded: Jenö Takács's toccata and fugue, opus 56 (1951), Saint-Saëns's six studies, opus 135, Robert Saxton's *Chacony* (dedicated to Fleisher and premiered by him at the Aldeburgh festival in 1988), and Brahms's transcription of the Bach *Chaconne;* then, after the intermission, Scriabin's *Prélude et nocturne*, opus 9, Felix Blumenfeld's *étude* in A-flat, opus 36, and Godowsky's "Symphonic metamorphoses on the Schatz-Walzer" from Johann Strauss's *The Gypsy Baron* afterward. The second half of the concert departed from the printed program, however, because the natives were restless; consequently Scriabin replaced both Lipatti's sonatina and Jean Hasse's *Silk Water* (another piece dedicated to, and premiered by, Fleisher).

The concert was a profoundly *sinister* spectacle, and the audience, mostly heavily rouged and voluble Fellini-esque old ladies in leopard coats, added to the circus atmosphere, as if the pianist belonged to a freak show—as a musical cousin of Thing from *The Addams Family,* or of "the beast with five fingers."[12] The

12. In Robert Florey's *The Beast with Five Fingers,* Victor Francen plays a virtuoso pianist whose right hand has been paralyzed. After his death, his severed left hand apparently continues to play the piano (specifically, the *Chaconne* from Bach's D minor violin partita, transcribed, in the film, by Robert Alda) and takes on a second career as a strangler.

In Alfred Hitchcock's *Rope,* the implicitly homosexual anti-hero, played by Farley Granger, is also a strangler as well as a pianist who plays the first of Poulenc's *Mouvements perpétuels.*

most disturbing aspect of the concert, however, was that the music itself attempted to sustain an illusion, aurally at any rate, that all of the works Fleisher played were actually written for both hands. In other words, the music was created to compensate for, but did not transcend, a limitation.

Perhaps not surprisingly, the best thing Fleisher played that day was, by way of an encore, his own transcription of Gershwin's song "The Man I Love"; a piece that spiritually suggested unfulfillment, incompletion, loss, in a way nothing else on the program did.

Later, Fleisher regained sufficient use of his right hand to play Mozart's A major concerto, K. 414, then the Brahms D minor concerto. Though he had attempted to play bimanually in 1982— with Franck's *Symphonic Variations*, which he had recorded in the 1950s—the improvement was only temporary. The spirit was wholly willing, but the flesh was not.

The Magician

James Gibbons Huneker, in his memoir *Steeplejack*, remembers a pianist and magician who went by the name of Robert Heller (1829–1878):

> Heller, whose real name was Palmer, and an Englishman, was an excellent pianist. A grand piano always stood on the stage surrounded by his infernal apparatus; cones and cabinets, glittering brass, and the complete paraphernalia of the successful prestidigitator. Heller played the operatic fantasias of Thalberg—then considered extremely difficult—with technical finish and musical taste. He had evidently studied in a good school and his touch sang on the keyboard. What he accomplished in the other craft I have forgotten.

An episode from the life of Liszt evokes the circus figure of the magician more obliquely.

In 1838 he was playing in Milan. Having been reproached for giving concerts that were "too serious," he decided to introduce the custom (then popular in Paris) of improvising on familiar melodies proposed by members of the audience and chosen by acclamation. In a letter written at this time, Liszt described "a lovely silver cup of exquisite workmanship, attributed to one of Cellini's most gifted pupils" into which the themes were to be placed, and from which he—like a magician pulling a rabbit from a hat—would draw them and read them aloud until the Milanese approved one. The first themes were the expected names of melodies by Bellini and Donizetti. "But then, to the audience's great amusement," Liszt wrote, "I read a carefully folded, unsigned note from a person who had not a moment's doubt about the towering superiority of his suggestion, 'The Cathedral of Milan.'" The Milanese did not choose this theme, however; nor did they choose "The Railroad." Liszt opened the last note.

> What do you think I read this time? One of life's most important concerns, and I was supposed to settle it in arpeggios! It was a subject which, if treated broadly, would call everything into question; religion as well as physiology, philosophy as well as political economy—namely, 'Is it better to marry or to remain single?' Not being able to answer that question with anything but an infinitely long sigh, I preferred to remind my audience of what a wise man once said: 'No matter what decision a person makes, whether to get married or to remain single, he is always bound to regret it.'

Prodigies

Little fellows in socks and shorts,
Beating their Broadwood pianofortes.
Little maidens in frill and frock,
Scraping away like one o'clock.

—*from a doggerel poem on prodigies* (Punch, 1893)

Though all great pianists are prodigies, not all prodigies are great pianists. Instead, musical history is littered with prodigies who, like Peter Pan, could not grow up, or who expired romantically and tragically during their prodigy years, or who simply disappeared. Károly (or Karl) Filtsch (called "Le Petit"), for instance, taught by Chopin and specially admired by Liszt, died of consumption in Venice not even three weeks shy of his fifteenth birthday, and was mourned across Europe.[13] I have been unable to

13. After hearing the boy play his E minor concerto, Chopin said, "Nobody has ever understood me as this child does, the most extraordinary thing I have ever experienced." Filtsch was a promising composer as well. The most substantial of his works rumored to exist, a piano concerto, has not been found.

learn if such "infant phenomena"—Shaw's term for prodigies—as Ada La-Face, Adeline de Germain (known in her time as "La Petite Reine du Piano"), Elisa Piquée (who at the age of ten composed a Galop for piano, which she dedicated to a Madame Ollion), Brahm Van den Berg (Shaw, who heard him play in 1890, saw him dressed on that occasion "in a white sailor suit which would not have been out of place in a kindergarten," even though Master Brahm was "nearly as big as Pavia"[14]), and Ornella Vannucci (b. 1921) were even alive beyond their prodigy years. The fact that one knows nothing of them, that they are mentioned in no contemporary history of the piano, suggests that the flame of their talent did not continue to burn brightly in maturity (assuming they actually reached it).

During the last decade of the twentieth century, only Kissin (b. 1971) seems to have managed to survive his prodigy years intact. As for Constantin Lifschitz (b. 1976), though he gave a fantastic performance of *Gaspard de la nuit* at La Scala when he was sixteen, recorded the *Goldberg* variations—*à la Gould*—while in his early twenties, then opened his first London recital (at Wigmore Hall) with Couperin's *Huitième Ordre,* his adult career has been wobbly: he does not yet seem to understand that wisdom and sobriety do not preclude joy and fire. Dimitris Sgouros (b. 1969), on the other hand, disappeared after earning some of the most spectacular praise imaginable during *his* prodigy years. (His adult recording of the Brahms concerti paid no tribute to his former glories.)

Understandably, former prodigies often have the least patience for current ones. Liszt, for instance, bristled against being treated like "the learned dog Munito" (1820-1830), a "matchless dog" who understood "equally well French and Italian, works out the letters of the alphabet, distinguishes colors, plays dominoes ... and is acquainted with the principles of geography and botany." ("Artists who *are* to be?" was Liszt's opinion of the breed—always excepting Filtsch.) According to Newman, Rosenthal (Liszt's only pupil at Tivoli during the autumn of 1878) once had a conversation along this line with a prodigy:

14. Not the city, but rather Isidore Pavia—another piano prodigy.

'So you are going to play to me?'
'Please sir, yes sir.'
'And what are you going to play?'
'Please sir, the "Tchaikovsky Concerto in B flat minor."'
'Oh that? And how old are you?'
'Please sir, four-and-a-half sir.'
'Four-and-a-half? Too old!'

Arrau told Joseph Horowitz that as a prodigy, "I became a sort of circus animal. Children of my age either thought I was something amazing, to be able to do such feats with my hands, or they thought I was funny, strange, not a normal person. These two reactions were awful—both of them." Hofmann, another sensational prodigy, was in the process of being thoroughly exploited (in fact, he played more than fifty concerts in the ten weeks subsequent to his American début), but was uniquely spared when the philanthropist Alfred Corning Clark paid fifty thousand dollars to his father on condition that Josef "retire" from the concert stage until his eighteenth birthday. (It was during this retirement that Hofmann returned to Europe and studied with Rubinstein.) Schumann's "predilection" for child prodigies, which he confessed in an 1834 article on Theodor Stein (a pianist then fourteen or fifteen years of age), remains almost unique. (Of course, Clara was a child prodigy when he fell in love with her; more significantly, he himself had *not* been one.)

The public's preoccupation with the mere fact of childhood achievement overshadows a more considered response to the prodigy's playing, not to mention concern for the degree to which early fame may damage him (or her). The prodigy thus becomes to the public what the child is to the pedophile: a being whose obsolescence is built in (*cf.* the eight-year-old Bibi in Mann's story "Das Wunderkind"). The prodigy is commonly portrayed at one of two extremes—as either a child or a miniature adult—and neither proposition is kind. After all, to be imprisoned in a childhood is no less cruel than to be deprived of one.

Helen Huang, for instance, was shown on the cover of her second recording—solo works by Mozart, Schumann, Debussy, and Villa-Lobos *For Children*—sitting on a piano bench alongside a new-looking stuffed animal as a sledgehammer reminder that, at least chronologically, she was still a child. (By contrast, the program for Vannucci's 1929 recital at the Sala Sgambati in Rome presents a photograph of the artist—who debuted in 1928, having begun to study the instrument only in 1927—holding a worn, clearly beloved doll.) By the time she made her third recording (concerti by Mendelssohn-Bartholdy and Mozart with Kurt Masur and the New York Philharmonic), on the other hand, Huang was being put forward as a miniature siren: on this cover, she wears a sleeveless blouse, and a jacket that falls suggestively from her shoulders: the shot incarnates that curious mixture of innocence and seduction that characterized Nabokov's *Lolita.* For all this, in the booklet notes to the recording, Andrea Hechtenberg emphasizes the normalcy of Huang's upbringing, observing that at "fifteen years old, she leads the life of a fairly typical teenager, holding long conversations on the phone with her friends, going swimming with them, watching films and undertaking lengthy shopping expeditions." What Hechtenberg neglects to observe is that typical teenagers do not play concerti with the Berlin Philharmonic; nor do they—one prays—have their clothes coaxed off of them by photographers.

Germaine, poor child, was represented as a siren from the start. In Paris I found a postcard of her aged six and a half and posed *comme ça:* her head is resting in her right hand (her right elbow being on the piano), while her left hand is on her left hip, in eerie anticipation of one of Mae West's famous postures; clearly intended to titillate those with a taste for what the Victorians called "unripe fruit." On the other hand, a photograph of Teresa Carreño taken when she was eight—about the time she played for Lincoln at the White House (and complained about the quality of the piano there)—captures a luminous and searching dignity worthy of the most mature artist.

The Hungarian virtuoso and composer Ervin Nyiregyházi—who was born in 1903, the same year as Arrau, Horowitz, and Serkin (this year was for pianists what 1685, the year J. S. Bach, Giustini, Händel and Domenico Scarlatti were born, was for composers)— was the subject of a 1916 book about the prodigy by Geza Révész, Director of Amsterdam's Psychological Laboratory). In the end, however, Nyiregyházi's adult life was far more fascinating than his childhood.

In 1918, Nyiregyházi played the Liszt A major concerto with Nikisch and the Berlin Philharmonic (he had made his debut with the orchestra in 1915, playing Beethoven's third), and substituted for Rachmaninov in Tchaikovsky's first concerto in Oslo. He gave his American debut, at Carnegie Hall, on 18 October 1920 playing Busoni's transcription of Bach's D minor toccata and fugue, Liszt's arrangement of Schubert's *Wanderer* fantasy, Scriabin's F-sharp major sonata and *Poème Satanique,* the Chopin *Barcarolle,* a Grieg nocturne, Leschetizky's "Heroic Etude," then Liszt's second *Petrarch* sonnet and first *Mephisto* waltz. Notwithstanding such auspicious opportunities, however, his performing career was over by 1925.

He settled in Los Angeles, composed, and supported himself by working as a film studio pianist and actor.[15] His hands doubled for Paul Henreid's in *Song of Love* and Cornel Wilde's in *Song to Remember,* the soundtracks for which were recorded, respectively, by Rubinstein and José Iturbi; his left hand was *The Beast with Five Fingers.* (He also wrote a monograph on Wilde.) Schoenberg, then living in Southern California, heard Nyiregyházi play at the house of a friend in 1935. Afterwards, the composer described the former prodigy's playing in a letter to Otto Klemperer as "a power of the will, capable of soaring over all imaginable difficulties in the realization of an idea. . . ." A collaboration between Nyiregyházi and Klemperer never resulted, however, because the pianist substituted the last movement of Chopin's B-flat minor sonata for the last movement of his B minor one (transposing it, of course) when auditioning for the conductor (who was, like Schnabel, a proponent of the new literalism). Nyiregyházi regarded the former movement as superior to the latter.

Then, in May 1973, he played Liszt's *Legends* ("Saint Francis of Assisi Preaching to the Birds" and "Saint Francis of Paola Walking on the Waves") at the Old First Church in San Francisco—a recording of this phenomenal occasion exists—to help defray the medical expenses of his ninth wife, Elsie. Despite the

---

15. Nyiregyházi was also the inspiration for David Leavitt's short story "Heaped Earth," first published (in an Italian translation) in the program book for a concert of American music at Milan's La Scala on 18 May 1998.

poor quality of the recording, and the sounds of traffic outside the church, Nyiregyházi's performance resonates with a powerfully religious majesty: he makes the *Legends* sound truly legendary, epic. During the last years of his life, he married a tenth time, and made incendiary (commercial) recordings of works by the Swiss composer Emile-Robert Blanchet (*Au jardin du vieux sérail*), Bortkiewicz (three *Travel Pictures*), Grieg, Tchaikovsky, and Liszt (whose very reincarnation he was once called), as well as of six of his own operatic transcriptions. He also found an especial appreciation for his art in Japan.

A most extraordinary life indeed.[16]

Animals

The following passage about a piano-playing monkey pays a debt to the hypothesis that if you seat a million monkeys at a million typewriters one of them will eventually write *A Tale of Two Cities*—a hypothesis that devalues Dickens by suggesting that he was little more than a labor-saving device for simians. Likewise this passage devalues virtuosi by suggesting that *their* art is merely the expression of an arbitrary, even autistic natural phenomenon. From Nicolas Slonimsky's *A Thing or Two about Music:*

> An unidentified newspaper clipping circa 1888 reports this incredible story. A music teacher in Kentucky taught a monkey to play the piano. The monkey developed such virtuosity that he could not only play piano duets in four hands with the aid of his four paws, but also learned to turn the pages with his tail. The dispatch said that the human pupils of the Kentucky professor could not even remotely emulate the monkey pianist.

Saint-Saëns placed *virtuosi*—in the limited sense of those who rush up and down the keyboard with no thought for tomorrow—among the fauna in his "Grande fantaisie zoölogique," *Carnival of the Animals.* Tellingly, he characterizes them as "Hémiones," or wild asses. "Pianistes" are part of his menagerie as well, but unlike "Hémiones" they cannot play even the simplest of scales without faltering.

16. I am indebted to Gregor Benko for sharing many chapters of Nyiregyházi's history with me.

The Clown

No virtuoso clowned around more than Pachmann, the arche-typal flamboyant homosexual.

Even the briefest sketch of his private life is fascinating. Pach-mann married the pianist Maggie Oakey, an innocent girl un-aware—before their wedding—of her husband's proclivities, and they had two sons who lived into adulthood, Adrian and Lionel (who also grew up to be homosexual, lived into his nineties, and died in Paris). After they divorced, Oakey married Fernand La-bori, who defended Alfred Dreyfus (of the famous affair). In his middle years, Pachmann took up with a charming young Italian named Francesco ("Cesco") Pallottelli, who grew rich off him, married, and became a fascist. (How strange that despite—or perhaps because of—its clownishness, Pachmann's life brushed against signal events of twentieth-century history; most notably, the rise of fascism and the emergence of a visible homosexual style!)

As Pachmann grew older, his concerts became ever more no-table for the antics he performed on stage rather than for his ac-tual playing: his adjustments to the piano stool and his running commentaries were legendary. He was also wont to demand the ejection of any ugly old ladies from the front rows of his audi-ences, and their replacement with "hunky" young men—and then would proceed to make eyes at them, dedicate perform-ances to them, blow kisses, and so on.

At his colleagues' concerts, he was famous for his carryings-on in the audience. At a Godowsky concert, "[H]e rushed to the stage at one point," Schonberg recounts in *The Great Pianists*. "'No, no, Leopold,' he said, to the vast amusement of the audi-ence and the fire-engine blush of Godowsky, 'you moost play it like so.' He played it like so, and then told the audience he wouldn't have given the demonstration for just any old pianist. 'But Godowsky,' he said, 'is ze zecond greatest liffing pianist.'"

For all his clowning around, however, Pachmann was once a superb pianist. Sorabji, in a short assessment titled "Pachmann and Chopin," wrote that before "extravagances and eccentrici-ties" overwhelmed his art, Pachmann's "playing of the smaller nocturnes, waltzes, études and mazurkas was exquisite." (In his article "How to Play Chopin," published in *The Etude* in October 1908, Pachmann showed that his words, too, could be lovely: of the third prelude, he wrote, "The melody is so smooth that it reminds me of oil floating on water, while a sort of zither accompaniment is running.") And Cardus, in "Chopin and Pianists," described his interpretations as "gem-like" (the phrase so famous from Pater)—a perfect description, in a way, since Pachmann would sometimes bring jewels to his concerts, hold them up for admiration, and then say, "You will forget them when you hear me play. Pachmann has even more color."

Here is the ultimate moment in the lives of the pianistic clowns, from Michel Tournier's "Jesu, Joy of Man's Desiring: A Christmas Story":

> Did a kind of miracle take place that evening under the big top in Urbino? The plan was that in the finale, after struggling through a piece of music as best he could, the unfortunate Gammon should witness the explosion of his piano, which would vomit out into the ring a vast array of hams, custard pies, and strings of black and white sausages. But something quite different occurred . . . when the most complete silence reigned, he began to play. With contemplative, meditative, fervent serenity he played *Jesu, Joy of Man's Desiring*, the Bach chorale that had soothed his student years. And the poor old circus piano, for all its gimmicks and gadgets, obeyed his hands marvellously. . . . A long silence prolonged the last note, as if the chorale were continuing in the beyond. Then, in the shimmering clouds of his myopia, the musician-clown saw the piano lid rising. It didn't explode. It didn't spew out sausages. It opened slowly like a huge, dark flower, and released a beautiful archangel with wings of light, the Archangel Raphael, the one who had been watching over him all his life and preventing him from quite becoming Gammon.[17]

* * *

17. Cziffra began his career, at the age of five, as a circus pianist. And like the pianist in Tournier's story, he, too, was prevented "from quite becoming Gammon." In his memoir *Cannons and Flowers*, he wrote, "I only ever felt truly alive and free when passing from darkness to light or on taking flight from a dingy prison cell like a firebird."

The final word on the circus in general, however, must come from the career of Liszt. Intellectuals are often drawn to the low, to the sullying, and he regarded the circus in just this way. At the same time, because he was both a supreme genius and a man of enormous moral power, he exploited the atmosphere of the circus (in his youth) as a means of preparation for the revelation of sublimity. And he did so with a thoroughness, a courage, and an aplomb attained by no other artist before or after him. Jean Chantavoine:

> At the end of a concert he had given in Prague in 1840, as the enthusiasm of his audience demanded an encore, for which they wanted him to play his *Ave Maria* (after Schubert), Liszt first played the *Hexaméron*. On further insistence, still rebellious, he embarked, not on the *Ave Maria* but on one of the most vertiginous of his bravura pieces: the [*Grand*] *Galop chromatique* and, by a transition as unexpected as it was elegant, continued with the *Ave Maria*. . . . The attraction of his personality lies precisely in that only he could pass from the *Galop chromatique* to the *Ave Maria* without disrupting the modulations and without playing any false notes.

Liszt proved once and for all that the artist, and not the place where he finds himself, is responsible for what he creates.

AOÛT.

Postcard for the month of
August from series *Histoire
du Costume (de Louis XVI au
Second Empire)*. (Drawing by
Gavarni, 1834.)

"Brilliant performance of a
sonata for twenty fingers,"
showing how lascivious
natures may be aroused by
playing the piano. (From *Le
Charivari* [Paris], Sunday, 4
October 1846.)

LES BONNES TÊTES MUSICALES.

Exécution brillante d'une sonate à vingt doigts.

"Cesco" Pallottelli and Vladimir de Pachmann.

Front of Pachmann
concert program.

REALE ACCADEMIA
FILARMONICA ROMANA
(ANNO C)
LUNEDÌ 23 FEBBRAIO 1920, ORE 21

CONCERTO

de
PACHMANN

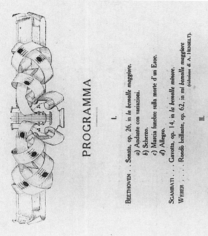

PROGRAMMA

I.

BEETHOVEN . . Sonata, op. 26, in *la bemolle maggiore*.
    a) Andante con variazioni.
    b) Scherzo.
    c) Marcia funebre sulla morte d'un Eroe.
    d) Allegro.

SCARLATTI . . . . Gavotta, op. 14, in *la bemolle minore*.
WEBER . . . . . Rondò brillante, op. 62, in *mi bemolle maggiore* (*riduzione di* A. HENSELT).

II.

MENDELSSOHN. Romanza senza parole, op. 102, n. 4, in *sol minore*.
SCHUMANN . . *Ende vom Sied*, op. 12, n. 8, in *fa maggiore*.
CHOPIN . . . . Notturno (opera postuma), op. 72, in *mi minore*.
    Mazurka, op. 24, n. 2, in *do maggiore*.
    Mazurka, op. 17, n. 1, in *si bemolle maggiore*.
    Secondo scherzo, op. 31, in *si bemolle minore*.

Agenzie:
LONDRA, NEW YORK, PARIGI, ecc.

Direzione Concerti:
F. PALLOTTELLI CORINALDESI
19, Piazza Cavour, Roma

VLADIMIRO DE PACHMANN

PHOTO. ELLIOT & HRY, LONDRA

VLADIMIRO DE PACHMANN nacque a Odessa il 27 luglio 1848. A 18 anni aveva già dato prova pubblica del suo talento. A Vienna perfezionò la sua cultura musicale studiando armonia e fuga con Antonio Bruckner. Indi iniziò quella carriera di concertista che dovevà condurlo a celebrità mondiale. Nel 1870 ebbe occasione di udire il grande Tausig, il quale molto lo impressionò con la sua tecnica, e lo annuò a maggiormente perfezionarsi. A 30 anni fu a Lipsia, ove diede un concerto sotto la direzione di Carlo Reinecke. A Parigi suonò nei concerti diretti da Pasdeloup, destando vivo entusiasmo. Da Parigi passò a Londra; e colà fu accolto con quella fervida simpatia che tuttora è viva per lui.

A Budapest conobbe Liszt, che tributò i più caldi elogi al giovane pianista, specialmente per la delicatezza del tocco. Liszt e che Pachmann furono spesso insieme; le due anime si compresero, e fu alla l'amicizia e l'ammirazione che legò de Pachmann al celebre musicista.

Nel 1890 si recò in America per un giro di 25 concerti, destando grande entusiasmo.

De Pachmann dette pure dei concerti in Italia. Dopo molti anni, egli ritorna nel nostro paese; e a Roma, quest'anno, ha destato vivissima commozione nell'eletto uditorio della capitale.

Interior of Pachmann program of 23 February 1920.

Josef Hofmann circa 1897 in
Berlin. (Courtesy Gregor
Benko.)

Adeline de Germain, the "Little
Queen of the Piano" at the age
of six and a half.

A. R. C.

SALA SGAMBATI

Martedì 28 Maggio 1929 - Ore 17,30 precise

CONCERTO
DELLA PIANISTA
ORNELLA VANNUCCI
sotto gli auspici
dell'Associazione fra i Toscani in Roma

PROGRAMMA

1. — MOZART . . . . — Fantasia in *re minore.*
   SCARLATTI . . . . . . — Sonata in *la.*
   HAYDN . . . . — Sonata in *re.*

2. — SCHUBERT . . . . . . — Impromptu.
   DEBUSSY . . . . — Serenata alla Bambola.
   ALBENIZ . . . . — Rumores de la Caleta.

3. — STORTI . . . . — Pifferata.
   SCHUBERT . . . . — Momento musicale.
   CHOPIN . . . . — Valse, op. 64 n. 1.
   CHOPIN . . . . — Impromptu Op. 66.

Pianoforte "Steinway & Sons,, Ditta Fornaciari (Corso Umberto I., 267)

ORNELLA VANNUCCI è nata a Livorno nel 1921.
Iniziati gli studi pianistici a Roma nel novembre del 1927 con la professoressa Celestina Poce Pane, dava il primo saggio pubblico nel giugno del 1928 ; e nel dicembre dello stesso anno si produceva in una audizione nella *Sala Maggiore* dell'Associazione fra Toscani in Roma destando il più vivo interesse, la più schietta ammirazione ed ottenendo un netto successo di pubblico e di stampa.

È proibito entrare nella Sala durante l'esecuzione dei pezzi.

P R E Z Z I :
POSTO IN SALA L. 12 — GALLERIA L. 6
I biglietti sono in vendita presso l'*Ufficio Viaggi Roesler Franz* - Via Condotti, 88; presso la Associazione fra i Toscani - Via dei Prefetti, Palazzo Piceni e al Botteghino della Sala all'ora del Concerto

Ai soci dell'Associazione fra i Toscani e loro famiglie i biglietti vengono ceduti rispettivamente a L. 8 e a L. 4.

Ornella Vannucci. Advertisement for a concert
in Rome on 28 May 1929.

Hazel Harrison in 1904. (Library of Congress.)

Paderewski's piano stool.

Glenn Gould on the
low stool that his
father built for him.
(Photograph © Hulton-
Deutsch Collection/
CORBIS.)

Lithograph of Beethoven from the
publishing house of Schumann's father:
Gebr. Schumann (Zwickau). (From *Bildnisse
der beruhmtesten Menscher aller Volker und Zeiten*
[1819, 1832].)

Soirée program listing
(in item 6) works
playing during the
1927 silent film
Beethoven. From a set
of postcards that
includes the scenes
on the next page.

CENTENAIRE de BEETHOVEN

THÉATRE DU TROCADÉRO

GALA CINEMATOGRAPHIQUE du 6 Avril 1927

———·ô·———

PROGRAMME

1. DANSE ARABE de LALO
   par l'Orchestre sous la direction de M. Paul FOSSE.

2. *A travers l'Afrique inconnue* (*film inédit*)
   (Mission en A. O. F. du Synchronisme Cinématique)
   CHEZ LES CONIAGUIS
   CHEZ LES BASSARIS
   CHEZ LES CERÈRES.

   Entr'acte

3. LÉONORE N° 3 Ouverture
   par l'Orchestre.

4. ORGUE .. .. ,, ... M. Marcel DUPRÉ

5. **BEETHOVEN**
   film réalisé à l'occasion du centenaire du grand musicien
   sur les lieux mêmes où il a vécu.
   (Édition du Synchronisme Cinématique)
   Son enfance... Sa gloire... Ses amours... Ses souffrances...
   Sa mort. F. KORTNER dans le rôle de Beethoven.

6. PRINCIPALES ŒUVRES de **BEETHOVEN**, exécutées
   pendant la projection du film :

Première Symphonie	Sixième Symphonie
Troisième Symphonie (Héroïque)	Fidelio (ouverture)
Cinquième Symphonie	Septuor (fragments)
Sonate pathétique.	

From *Beethoven:* "Beethoven et son maître Joseph Haydn,"

"Les amours de Beethoven et de la comtesse Guicciardi,"

and "Beethoven composant sa neuvième symphonie."

WIGMORE HALL
WIGMORE STREET, W.1

𝔅𝔢𝔢𝔱𝔥𝔬𝔳𝔢𝔫 𝔑𝔢𝔠𝔦𝔱𝔞𝔩

Saturday, Sept. 26th
at 2.30 p.m.

RE-APPEARANCE OF . . . . .

LAMOND

THE GREATEST LIVING EXPONENT OF BEETHOVEN

TICKETS (including Tax) **Reserved 7/6 and 5/-, Unreserved 2/6**

May be obtained at the Box-Office, Wigmore Hall; usual Ticket Offices and

IBBS & TILLETT, 124, Wigmore Street, W.1

Telephone : Welbeck 2325 (3 lines)   Ticket Office :   Welbeck 8418
Telegrams : " Organol, Wesdo, London "   Hours 10—1 2—5 Sats: 10—12

VAIL AND CO. LTD., E.C.1   For Programme P.T.O.

Front of advertisement for Frederic Lamond concert
in London, 26 September 1942.

Programme

BEETHOVEN

Sonata, B flat major, Op. 106

(Grand Sonata for the Hammerclavier)

Allegro—Scherzo, Assai Vivace—Adagio—Fuga à re voce,

Andante favori

Sonata pathetique, C minor, Op. 13

Grave.   Allegro di molto e con brio—Adagio cantabile—
Rondo. Allegro.

Rondo, Op. 51, No. 2

Sonata, F minor, Op. 57 (Appassionata)

Allegro assai—Andante con moto—Allegro ma non troppo.

Bösendorfer Pianoforte

Back of Lamond advertisement.

WIGMORE HALL
WIGMORE STREET. W. 1

5 Pianoforte Recitals

Wednesday, Feb.   2, at 8.30

Thursday,   „   10 „ 3

Tuesday,   „   22 „ 8.30

Thursday, March 3 „ 3

Thursday,   „   17 „ 8.30

LEFF POUISHNOFF
THE RUSSIAN PIANIST   (First Appearance in England)

CHAPPELL CONCERT GRAND PIANOFORTE

TICKETS (including Tax) : 12/-, 8/6 & 5/9   Admission, 3/-
May be obtained from the BOX OFFICE, WIGMORE HALL (Mayfair 1282); the Usual Agents; and of
The E. L. ROBINSON DIRECTION, Empire House, 175, Piccadilly, W.1 'Phone : Ger. 6433

P.T.O.

From Leff Pouishnoff's English début—with a five-concert series in February and March 1921.

Vladimir Horowitz. Portrait by Eugen Spiro (American,
1874–1972)—inscribed by the artist on 23 April 1945.

May 8, 1973

A Piano Recital of Transcriptions by Rachmaninoff and Liszt

JORGE BOLET, piano

Program

TRANSCRIPTIONS BY SERGEI RACHMANINOFF (1873-1943)
(Played in Commemoration of the 100th Anniversary of the Composer's Birth)

JOHANN SEBASTIAN BACH (1685-1750)
Prelude, from Partita No. 3 in E Major for Unaccompanied Violin

GEORGES BIZET (1838-1875)
Menuet, from *L'Arlésienne*

VASILY RACHMANINOFF (ca. 1842-1916)
Polka

MODEST MUSSORGSKY (1839-1881)
Hopak, from *Sorotchinsky Fair*

PETER ILYITCH TCHAIKOWSKY (1840-1893)
Lullaby

NIKOLAI RIMSKY-KORSAKOV (1844-1908)
Flight of the Bumblebee, from *Tsar Saltan*

FELIX MENDELSSOHN (1809-1847)
Scherzo, from Incidental Music to *A Midsummer Night's Dream*

FRITZ KREISLER (1875-1962)
Liebesleid (Love's Sorrow)
Liebesfreud (Love's Joy)

INTERMISSION

TRANSCRIPTIONS BY FRANZ LISZT (1811-1886)

FRANZ LISZT
Sonnet 47 by Petrarch
Sonnet 104 by Petrarch
Sonnet 123 by Petrarch

RICHARD WAGNER (1813-1883)
Overture to *Tannhauser*

The Baldwin Concert Grand has been provided through the courtesy of The Baldwin Music Center

From Romantic Festival VI, Butler University,
Indianapolis. (Courtesy Frank Cooper.)

AMICI DELLA MUSICA
FIRENZE

TEATRO DELLA PERGOLA
Venerdì 24 marzo 1995 - ore 21

KRYSTIAN ZIMERMAN
pianoforte

C. DEBUSSY   — *Images (I serie)*
               Reflets dans l'eau
               Hommage à Rameau
               Mouvement

A. WEBERN   — *Kinderstück (H. 262)*

J.S. BACH   — *Partita n. 2 in do minore, BWV 826*
               Sinfonia (Grave Adagio, Andante, [Allegro])
               Allemanda
               Corrente
               Sarabanda
               Rondeaux
               Capriccio

K. SZYMANOWSKI — *Studio in si bemolle minore, op. 4 n. 3*

A. WEBERN   — *Klavierstück, op. post. 43*

F. CHOPIN   — *Sonata n. 2 in si bemolle, op. 35 («Marcia funebre»)*
               Grave, Doppio movimento
               Scherzo
               Marcia funebre (Lento)
               Finale (Presto)

encores   *Webern*
          Bach - Zimerman   *Passacaglia*
                      (BWV 532)

A notable encore.

Sviatoslav Richter, with Shostakovich score on the piano.
(Photographer unknown. Private collection.)

6.

The Nature of the Bis

A strange custom, the *bis*—a bit like the surprise
in the Easter egg. Only children want the surprise
more than the egg. It seems that sometimes, at the
end of a concert, we all become children once
again.

— *Piero Rattalino*

The most ritualistic part of the virtuoso recital is the encore; the
ritual conferring now a benediction (Hess and Lipatti playing
"Jesu, Joy of Man's Desiring"), now the delight of transcendental
virtuosity (Horowitz playing Moszkowski, or Pogorelich *Islamey*).
Whatever the nature of the *bis*, however—whether it extends or
fulfills the spirit of the formal program, belongs to an altogether
different order, or repeats the last work of the concert, which
is what *bis* ("twice") actually means (this was often Richter's
practice)—it is a gift to those who remain, applauding, in the
theater.

The most wonderful concert of my concertgoing life for its
pendant of encores was a recital by Kissin in Bologna in April
1994. He stepped smartly onto the stage at 9:00 p.m. and finished
his *thirteenth* encore, Liszt's "Harmonies du soir," at thirty-five minutes past midnight.[1] The audience, conscious that it was both wit-

1. The other twelve were Liszt's "Waldesrauschen," Chopin's *Grand-Valse* in
A-flat, Schubert-Tausig's *Marche-militaire*, Chopin's F minor mazurka, opus 68 and
E minor waltz, opus posthumous, Bach-Kempff's *Siciliano*, Tchaikovsky's *Nata-
Valse*, Rachmaninov's prelude opus 23, no. 2, Schubert's A minor sonata, opus 143
(third movement) and B major sonata, opus 147 (second movement), Liszt's "La
leggierezza" and tenth *Transcendental* study.

nessing and bringing about a minor piece of musical history, called, *"Grazie"* ("Thank you"), not *"Bis,"* when Kissin returned to the stage—more than forty times—aware that what we were witnessing was a phenomenon that by century's end was almost extinct: virtuoso exuberance.

A few months later in Florence, after he played the Rachmaninov third (as well as, for encores, Rachmaninov's prelude opus 23, no. 2 and Alan Richardson's transcription of the same composer's *Vocalise*), I sent a note to Kissin asking him if he had ever played so many encores as he did in Bologna. "I only prepared three encores," he wrote; "the rest I was just playing from the memory. I had no other concert like that in my life—but, I think, it's worth being a musician just for one such concert."

Alas, encores rarely follow performances of the last three Beethoven or Schubert sonatas—as if those pieces constitute a "last word" after which nothing more can be said. The fact is, Beethoven wrote the ninth symphony, *Missa Solemnis, Diabelli* variations (Hildebrandt described them as "the most volcanic, bizarre, rugged, ironic, romantic and tempestuous compositions that Beethoven ever wrung from his Broadwood"), opus 126 bagatelles, and string quartets opp. 127, 130-132, and 135 after his last piano sonata. The impulse to silence a composer is extremely violent.

Schiff is an admirable dissenter from the "no encore" policy practiced by many of his colleagues and predecessors. (Schnabel never played them, and Toscanini, who frowned upon soloists giving encores after concerti, maintained that if he were a pianist he—like Schnabel—would not play them after recitals either.) For instance, in Florence he ended a beautiful six-concert traversal of Schubert's sonatas with the B-flat major, D. 960—preceded by the sonatas in E-flat major, D. 568 (opus posthumous 122) and F minor, D. 625/505 (the strangest of all Schubert's piano works)—then played two encores: the first of three piano pieces, D. 946, and the second of the opus 90 impromptus. Having many times before been left in silence to ponder this sonata (or Beethoven's opus 111) after a performance that hardly gave one anything to ponder, I was surprised that Schiff played encores; but more than surprised, I was moved. Silence after the performance of such works emphasizes their lastness—"after this, there was nothing more"—but it also narrows the view of the composer's creative life: there were no sonatas after this one, of course, but so much astonishing music came *before* it! In challenging a convention, Schiff's concert gave expression to the whole of the composer's genius, so that the end was not the end at all, but an opportunity to begin to play the music all over again. He gave the lie to the idea that the virtuoso deforms the composer's legacy; instead, he proved that the virtuoso affirms and renews it. At the same time, Schiff hearkened back to a more innocent era of Schubert performance.

The April 1907 issue of *The Musician* proposed programs for three Schubert recitals, and although the B-flat major sonata is present on the third, it starts things off. (Tausig's transcription of the *Marche-militaire* brings the program to a close.) These three programs show what an earlier time took from Schubert. A century ago there was obviously no shame in playing—and in listening to—Schubert's music through the lens of a virtuoso transcription or arrangement; constructions which often projected the music into the concert hall more effectively than the originals themselves could have done. (Schubert, unlike Beethoven or Liszt, was not himself a virtuoso pianist.) The fact that these programs do not share the present day's tendency toward encyclopedism is felicitous; as if, a century ago, there was all the time in the world to play Schubert's music. Now, because time may be running out, only the principal monuments (purged of later virtuoso contributions) can be maintained.

Such recitals as these are unique to a virtuoso past, one that was as naive as it was urbane. Schnabel and Brendel have stripped Schubert of his charm so that he is no longer the feckless lover and singer (in the poetic sense) who played music with his friends, but the isolated narrator of *Winterreise*. Rather than being loved as a warm living being, he is like Eliot's "patient etherized upon a table." I do not begin to suggest that the very real aspect of terror in Schubert's music be neglected—it is as essential to it as is the Viennese waltz—yet I long for the Romantic virtuoso's alertness to the immediate appeal of its loveliness. It may be that if virtuosi actually played hyphenated Schu-

First Program
I. Sonata in A minor, opus 42
II. Impromptu in C minor, opus 90, no. 1
Impromptu in G ("Elegie"), opus 90, no. 3[2]
Sonata in G major, opus 78 (*Menuetto*)
Adagio and *Rondo* in E major, opus [post.] 1453[3]
III. *Moments Musicaux* nos. 1, 2, and 3, opus 94
"Wohin?" [from *Die schöne Müllerin*] and "Die Forelle" (trans. Stephen Heller)

Second Program
I. Fantasie, opus 15
II. Impromptu in E-flat, opus 90, no. 2
Scherzo (no. 4 of *Fünf Klavierstücke*, opus post.)
Sonata in A major, opus 120 (*Andante*)
Impromptu in B-flat, opus 142, no. 3
III. Five Songs Transcriptions (trans. Liszt):
"Auf dem Wasser zu singen," "Du bist die Ruh," "Am Meer," "Horch, horch! die Lerch," and "Erlkönig"

Third Program
I. Sonata in B-flat, opus post.
II. Impromptu in F minor, opus 142, no. 1
Impromptu in A-flat, opus 90, no. 4
Moments Musicaux nos. 4, 5, and 6, opus 94
Valse Caprice (*Soirée de Vienne* no. 6, trans. Liszt)
III. *Impromptu à la Hongroise* and *March* (trans. Xavier Scharwenka)
"Ständchen" (trans. Liszt)
Marche-militaire (trans. Tausig)

---

2. This impromptu was actually written in the key of G-flat. Hans von Bülow recast it into G major. Liszt's transcription—of which there is an exquisite recording by Emil von Sauer—is also in G major.
3. Otto Erich Deutsch assigned these works the numbers 505 and 506, respectively, in his catalogue of Schubert's works.

bert they would be led back to the *anima* of Romantic piano playing.

In Wilde's dialogue *The Critic as Artist*, Earnest says, "If a man's work is easy to understand, an explanation is unnecessary. . . ." Gilbert replies, "And if his work is incomprehensible, an explanation is wicked."

7.

"The Colour of Classics"

The standards of the virtuoso as an individual are not, in the case of recordings, those that necessarily prevail. Increasingly, those of the record label dominate, and none claims so God-like a power over the recordings that bear its seal as Deutsche Grammophon. Thus, DGG's recitals catalogue reads, "Pianists set on a career make recordings. Pianists set on a world career make recordings for Deutsche Grammophon." (Later, when the catalogue explained that Horowitz came to the label late in his life, I felt almost as if I were reading a conversion story.) Does DGG expect us to believe that any pianist—any virtuoso—who does not record for the Yellow Label is *not* set on a "world career," or that the opportunity to make recordings for DGG is somehow elective? Unless I am mistaken, the catalogue is saying that DGG will offer me the opportunity to record Brahms's second concerto and Liszt's *Totentanz* (as soloist) with the Vienna Philharmonic— my oldest, fondest, and wildest dream—if only I affirm that I am "set on a world career." All right, then, I am. And I would like for Carlos Kleiber to conduct.

Instead of acknowledging that it owes its reputation to the artists who record for it, DGG proposes that simply by lending its yellow imprimatur to a recording—"The Colour of Classics" is its centennial slogan—it imparts not only a certain status but also a certain quality. Are Jean-Luc Luisada and Anatol Ugorski and Lilya Zilberstein superior to Arrau, or Ashkenazy (in his youth), or Bolet, or Egorov, or Katchen, or Lipatti, or Rubinstein, or Peter Serkin, or Zacharias—simply because the former record for DGG? Not even one of these three DGG pianists has made a really distinguished recording for the yellow label. Luisada, in fact, has been let go, and I cannot but wonder if Ugorski and Zilberstein are not far behind him. Ugorski's version of the Brahms sonatas—and equally Messiaen's *Catalogue d'oiseaux*—is among the most irritating piano playing ever preserved for hapless posterity. (And yet, his recording of the Scriabin concerto with Boulez and the Chicago Symphony Orchestra is excellent.) DGG has done neither Zilberstein nor the public any favors by recording her in Rachmaninov concerti and Brahms's late *Klavierstücke*, in French repertoire and a Liszt recital fiercely alien to either charm or repose.

DGG can also be brutally commercial. Berman recorded for DGG during the 1970s, but was unceremoniously dumped from its roster, not for artistic reasons but because, having been accused of fomenting anti-Soviet propaganda, he was refused permission to travel beyond the iron curtain for four years. Quite simply, DGG did not think that it paid to wait so long for him to fulfill its plans for him. (Berman now records for the Italian label Phoenix, and declares himself far happier there.) Zimerman began recording for DGG after he won the Chopin competition, but returned his contract because he was not given the artistic control over his recordings that he considered essential. Only when these controls were ceded to him did he resume recording. Later, DGG craftily co-opted Zimerman's perfectionism by labeling his recording of the Ravel piano concerti with Boulez—a CD whose release the pianist repeatedly postponed—"The Art of the Uncompromising."

* * *

The Woman Who Never Lived

On what would have been Liszt's ninety-second birthday, Miss Henriette Hutchens became the first black woman to play a piano concerto—in fact, she played two concerti—with the Berlin Philharmonic.

She had been born in Natchez, Mississippi, to former slaves in 1885. As is well known, many emancipated slaves continued to work for the families that had bought them (or their forbears) and took the sur-

name of those families as well. Henriette's parents were among these: her mother, Pecania, worked in the Hutchens's mansion (in the Greek revival style) as a cook; her father, whose left arm had withered after he was bitten by a rattlesnake in the 1850s, as a groom. The house in which they lived was composed of only two rooms, with a small porch off the front, yet it was decent and well-kept—and remembered by the pianist for the pink crape myrtle tree that grew between it and a neighboring house.

Hutchens showed her musical aptitude at the age of two. She sang constantly (and well), and therefore was noticed by the Ole Miss (the planter's wife). A musical amateur who had heard Liszt play in Paris during her youth, the Ole Miss—Hutchens recalled in a rare interview decades later—gave her the benefit of all the musical knowledge she possessed. This took the form of thrice-weekly piano lessons in the mansion's music room, the other occupants of which were a harp (which the little girl puzzled over, wondering how even in heaven angels could play such large instruments), a harmonium, a violin, and a banjo (which the master of the house picked up from time to time).

The story of any prodigy is marked by an almost impossible bit of good fortune, and so it was with Hutchens. Natchez, being both a phenomenally rich town before the war as well as a stop for boats running between New Orleans and Memphis, was visited by many celebrated artists. One such was Louis Moreau Gottschalk, America's first native-born virtuoso and author of the immensely popular Louisiana trilogy *("Bamboula," "La Savane," and "La Bananier"). He had played in Natchez just before the end of the war, and there had an affair with the French-born wife of a local planter. The woman conceived a child, but miscarried in the fifth month of her pregnancy and took this event as a judgment from God. Young Henriette was a godsend to her: the woman saw the girl as one who, guided properly, might become an artist as great as her lover. In this way, she would expunge the blot of her sin.*

It happened, then, that in 1891 Willie-Marie Cloud set sail for France with Henriette Hutchens. The girl was destined for the Conservatoire in Paris (where Gottschalk had studied), and a fame that, though once almost universal, is now all but obscure.

Although Hutchens was brought to the attention of Debussy—who delighted in her performance of his "Minstrels," for though he had never visited the United States, he had a Romantic image of its South—much hardship was to attend the formation of "La Perle Noire." Because she

*was young, learning French was only moderately difficult for her. Ini-
tially, she suffered most in her classes with Louis Diémer at the Conservatoire. Diémer, who had succeeded Marmontel at the Conservatoire
in 1887, was immensely wealthy (by marriage) and famous as "the king
of the scale and trill." He was not a universally admired musician—
Mark Hambourg described him as a "dry-as-dust player with a hard
rattling tone"—yet his pupils included, in addition to Hutchens, the
greatest French-born musicians of the first half of the twentieth century:
Casadesus, Ciampi, Cortot, Dupré, Lévy, Lortat, and Risler.*

*Imagine how the girl must have felt those first months in Paris, a
city so vast that all of Natchez would have filled no more than two
arrondissements! Her clothes were beautiful. She saw snow for the
first time.*

Here I have tried to imagine a scenario that would have allowed
a musically gifted black youth in the nineteenth century to develop as a pianist. The improbability of my invention, however, illustrates less the absence of practical opportunity at that time
than the fact that the idea of a serious black musician had not yet
occurred to most people—in either Paris or the United States.
Too often, it still does not. Thus a recent history of the piano suggests that early keyboard instruments had black lower keys in
order to "display to greater advantage the white hands of the performer."

Among all the solo artists on DGG's roster, I've not been able to
identify a single one who is black. Yet the absence—or at most
the minor presence—of black instrumentalists is not unique to
DGG. Instead, for the most dramatic illustration of the condition
of these musicians, one must look to the cover of a book: the Penguin 60 edition of *Let Them Call It Jazz* (three stories by Jean
Rhys). The cover pictures a black man playing the piano; not a
jazz pianist such as Earl "Fatha" Hines, Thelonious Monk, "Jelly
Roll" Morton, Bud Powell, Art Tatum, Cecil Taylor, or Teddy Wilson, for example, but André Watts. In one shot, Penguin managed to negate both the eminence of black jazz pianists and the
achievement of a small group of black classical pianists.

No black women have achieved major international careers
as classical pianists; indeed, the list of black women pianists is

a short one: Armenta Adams, Nerine Barrett, Monica Gaylord, Helen Hagan, Hazel (or Hazelda) Harrison (she played the Chopin E minor and Grieg A minor concerti with the Berlin Philharmonic, conducted by August Scharrer, on 22 October 1904), Natalie Hinderas, Philippa Duke Schuyler, Vivian Scott, Thomasina Talley, Flora Thompson (in 1935, the first black pianist to give a Town Hall [New York] recital), Lois Towles, Althea Waites, and Frances Walker (she played a program of music entirely by black composers at Carnegie Recital Hall in 1975) have achieved the most distinction. Equally small is the group of well-known black male classical pianists: Leon Bates, Samuel Dilworth-Leslie, Eugene Haynes, Raymond Jackson, Keith Jarrett, Robert Jordan, Matthew Kennedy, William Grant Naboré, Awadagin Pratt, George Walker (better known as a composer, he won the 1996 Pulitzer Prize in music), Watts, and, finally, Terrence Wilson, a former "New York City delinquent" (to quote from the March 1998 *Diapason* magazine) now studying at the Juilliard School and playing concerts internationally.[1] (Jarrett records for ECM, Pratt for EMI, and Watts, after time at Columbia and then EMI, for Telarc.)

I remember an episode of the sitcom *Bewitched* in which Tabatha, who has begun to take piano lessons, is magically transformed from a beginner into a virtuoso by her impatient grandmother, Endora. To the consternation of her parents, who want for her to play only as well as a mortal girl can, she plays Chopin's *Heroic* polonaise. (This is the opposite of the story *Sparky's Magic Piano,* in which the instrument itself dispenses virtuosity—until, that is, Sparky becomes an insufferably arrogant and ungrateful brat.) The plot of the *Bewitched* episode revolves around the plans of her teacher (Johann Sebastian Monroe, played by Jonathan Harris—Dr. Smith from *Lost in Space*), who believes her to be a genuine child prodigy. At the end, Endora's spell on Tabatha is lifted, and a true prodigy is found: the son of the black janitor at a high school. The young man plays Liszt's third *Liebestraum*

---

1. Thomas Greene Bethune, or "Blind Tom," was a piano-playing idiot savant born into slavery in 1848 who, at the age of eight, was billed as "The Greatest Musical Prodigy Since Mozart." He played throughout the United States and Europe, and died in 1908.

for the teacher, and—because it is television—all ends well. Once again, talent and practice are asserted over the magical and non-human and spellbinding.

As for the Liszt-playing lad (Gerald Edwards), I have often wondered if in real life he did go on—by magic or through practice—to become a virtuoso.

OF PARIS

For a Southerner, Paris is the most magical and haunting of European cities. And once upon a time Paris was at the center of my love for the piano.

I first went to Paris in May 1982, just a few days after I heard Horowitz play in London. Apart from the Louvre and the inevitable Eiffel Tower, I went to Père Lachaise to see the tomb of Chopin, to the Parc Monceau to see the monument to Chopin, and to the houses where Chopin lived and the one where he died. Chopin was not the only composer in my Panthéon at the time, however: I was a frank partisan of Ravel, of Saint-Saëns (his second and fourth concerti), of D'Indy's *Symphonie sur un chant montagnard français*, of Franck's *Variations symphoniques* (the recording by Casadesus with Ormandy and the Philadelphia Orchestra) and *Prélude, chorale et fugue* (Rubinstein's recording), and, no less passionately, of Fauré (the thirteenth nocturne).

The Paris of Gertrude Stein and Picasso appealed to me not at all. I wanted the Paris that I had seen in a *National Geographic* article on the City of Light, the one I had seen in a series of documentaries about Arthur Rubinstein (who lived on Avenue Foch). The Paris that appealed to me was one I extrapolated from the photographs in my college French book: cafés and pastry shops and book stalls along the Seine. It was the Paris of falling in love with a young Frenchman and of making love in a grand old Hausmann apartment. Such a city could not be assembled in a few days, so I set about trying to find a way to live there.

Back in Florida, I conceived the ambition of studying at the Conservatoire; an ambition encouraged by Ilana Vered, whom I had heard play both of the Ravel concerti in a concert about that time and who had studied at the Conservatoire herself. (Liszt had attempted to gain admission to the Conservatoire as well, but was turned away by Cherubini, the director, on the grounds that he was a foreigner.) Although I wrote away for the application, I put it aside when it arrived and never completed it. I spoke French well at the time, so I next wrote to the Sorbonne. The application arrived, and this too I set aside.

Thereafter I went devotedly to a West Palm Beach theater that showed foreign films, particularly films in French. I saw two that fueled the nostalgia for my abandoned pianistic career in Paris. *Practice Makes Perfect* concerned the relationship between a middle-aged pianist and a beautiful woman whom he had not married. (This was where I first heard the "Intermezzo" from Schumann's *Faschingsschwank aus Wien*.) *Heart to Heart* was not actually about music, yet the soundtrack included the second movement of Mozart's A major concerto (the recording by Pollini with Böhm and the Vienna Philharmonic). This was the first piece by Mozart that I truly loved, and it remains one of the few. And now lines begin to form circles: I could not find the recording used in the film, only one by Vered. It was coupled with the C major concerto, K. 467, but it was the A major to which I listened; and always, in truth, disappointedly. Though she encouraged my ambition to study at the Conservatoire, she was no Pollini.

After all this, Paris slowly paled. The next year I fell in love for the first time with a man, an American cellist. I fell into that relationship headlong and disastrously, endowing him with passions and abilities and virtues that he did not possess. My cellist, like Paris, was what I made him, and our months together took me a decade to get over. Through no fault of his, I find that I still hate him for so wedding music with personal failure that for a long time music itself pained me; and not only the music he played (at the time, a Britten suite and the Carter sonata), but the music we had shared on a Walkman (he would listen from the left earphone, and I from the right) and, later, on his stereo. ("Our song" was the Chopin cello sonata, in particular the trio of the scherzo, played by Argerich and Rostropovich.)

As it happened, our common life flew to pieces before we could see Paris together; one of the few blessings we had. Although I had to turn away from music, Paris remained a fantastic place in my imagination. It was with David that I finally heard Chopin in Paris, with David that I went to Père Lachaise, to pay homage to Chopin again, and now to Proust and Wilde as well, David with whom I listen to the French composers, who allow me to believe that this implausible world has grace and verve and beauty.

8.
Some Virtuosi in Literature

While no intelligent soul would claim a familiarity with a few paintings by Caravaggio or three novels by Faulkner as a basis for authoritative responses to painting or literature in general, a familiarity with a dozen "serious" pieces of music suffices today as musical literacy—as if music were somehow a less important art. Shaw, however, had no hesitation in writing,

> if you do not know Die Zauberflöte, if you have never soared into the heaven where they sing the choral ending of the Ninth Symphony, if Der Ring des Nibelungen is nothing to you but a newspaper phrase, then you are an ignoramus, however eagerly you may pore in your darkened library over the mere printed labels of those wonders that can only be communicated by the transubstantiation of pure feeling [into] musical tone.

Forster was another literary man sustained by music. In the essay "Not Listening to Music" (in *Two Cheers for Democracy*) he wrote that music "seems to be more 'real' than anything, and to survive when the rest of civilization decays"—but his is the minority view of the humanist and the musical amateur. He held music above the uses that can be made of it—by academics, as material for papers and conferences; by students, as a humanities credit—and reverenced the private gifts it bestows upon common life.

Literature is often aloof from music in a way that music is rarely aloof from literature. Works with musical titles such as Eliot's *Four Quartets* frequently have nothing to do with music proper, while for a number of writers music is only a costume in which to dress extra-musical preoccupations. One need only compare Wendell Kretschmar's lecture on Beethoven in Mann's *Doctor Faustus* with Proust's ecstatic description of listening to the Vinteuil Septet in *In Search of Lost Time* to recognize the difference between a static "use" of music and a passionate literary response.

The male virtuoso pianist has been an attractive figure to a handful of novelists,[1] though often these portrayals have availed themselves of clichés. Novels that feature virtuosi include Fred Mustard Stewart's *The Mephisto Waltz*, in which the hero makes a pact with the devil for his virtuosity; Frank Conroy's *Body & Soul*, a success story worthy of Horatio Alger; and Bernice Rubens's *Madame Sousatzka*, a melodrama of student-teacher-mother angst that was improved upon greatly in John Schlesinger's film adaptation.

In Andrew Solomon's *A Stone Boat*, the pianist protagonist must stand in for the autobiographical writer figure. Although Solomon makes his alter ego a virtuoso, the glimpses that he gives us of his musical life demonstrate an extreme ignorance of piano repertoire and playing. In one instance, the hero practices on a portable electric keyboard: "[T]he keys were too oddly sprung to work out subtle questions of phrasing," he tells us, "but I could at least drum through scales, negotiate fingering, and memorize new pieces"—one of these a Chopin nocturne. In another, during an all-Mozart recital in London, he programs a "divertimento" regardless of the fact that Mozart wrote no divertimenti for the instrument. (Likewise, his encore is "a light early Beethoven prelude" regardless of the fact that Beethoven wrote no preludes.) Finally, in Russia, where he plays Rachmaninov's second concerto, "a stout woman," moved by the sadness of

1. Stories about piano players are generally more varied of theme than novels about them. William Boyd's "Fantasia on a Favourite Waltz," Deborah Eisenberg's "Someone to Talk To," Louise Erdrich's "Woman Playing Chopin Naked," Forster's "Co-ordination," James Hamilton Paterson's "Sidonie Kleist," Felisberto Hernandez's "My First Concert," Wolfgang Hildesheimer's "Westcotte's Rise and Fall," Isherwood's "On Ruegen Island (Summer 1931)," Leavitt's "Heaped Earth," Mann's "Das Wunderkind," Maugham's "The Alien Corn," Nabokov's "Bachmann," Amy Tan's "Two Kinds," Tournier's "Jesu, Joy of Man's Desiring," and Eudora Welty's "June Recital" cover more territory than any equal number of novels.

his playing, comes up to him afterwards and tells him that she worked as a housekeeper to Rachmaninov. This woman would have to be old as well as stout since Rachmaninov left Russia in 1917—he made his last appearance as pianist there on 5 September—and never returned.

Solomon portrays his hero's life with no greater accuracy. A high degree of glamour attaches itself to the fictional pianist's career, which is highly artificial. During the course of the novel he plays in no fewer than three festivals. He also has an ideal recording contract, rarely practices, is very rich, remains indifferent to bad reviews (for all of his concerts are reviewed), never gets hemorrhoids (a curse of those in the sitting professions). His recording company has infinite patience for his personal tragedies; even the music itself has infinite patience for—and capacity to embrace—his personal tragedies.

This is, quite simply, a fantasy. Most likely it will not be in Paris (or in the recording studio) that you play the *Gaspard de la nuit* of your career, but in Austin, Texas. Yet this pianist does not play in Austin: each of his concerts seems to happen in an important place—Liszt in Paris, Schubert in Berlin, a "funny recital in Budapest." Rachmaninov's last concert, on the contrary, was in Knoxville, Tennessee; Hofmann's at Camp Wigwam, Harrison, Maine (1947); Lipatti's in Besançon, France; Backhaus's in Ossiach, Austria (28 June 1969); Youri Egorov's in Maastricht, The Netherlands; Richter's (apparently) in provincial Germany; Liszt's, excluding those concerts he gave for charitable causes after 1847 (the last of his eight "Years of Transcendental Execution"), in Elizabetgrad, in the Ukraine.

Solomon embroiders an art that he loves but does not understand, and he gets away with it because he is so intelligent about other things. Still, that "light early Beethoven prelude" glares. Not only does he look ridiculous for writing that, so do the many people who read his book in manuscript without noticing the invention; the acknowledgments list twenty-six.

Even as it pays nominal tribute to the figure of the virtuoso, *A Stone Boat* is ostentatious proof of culturally sanctioned, or at least culturally tolerated, musical illiteracy.

* * *

The Challoners, one of E. F. Benson's several homosexually encoded novels, is in its essentials the story of a father and his eventual acceptance of the decisions of his children: Helen marries an
atheist, while Martin is a virtuoso pianist who converts from An-
glicanism (his father is a clergyman in the C of E) to Catholicism.
Martin is at the center of this novel, wherein the veneration of
woman—in his case, of Stella—and the affirmation of the family
are the external forces against which he is compelled to assert his
devotion to music: stand-ins for homosexuality. (Though *The
Challoners* cannot be read as autobiography, Benson himself was
homosexual—as were his brothers Arthur and Hugh. Like the
fictional Martin's father, moreover, Benson's father, Edward White
Benson, became Archbishop of Canterbury and was, as Penelope
Fitzgerald described him, "integrity itself, a mighty force always
heading the same way, excluding other opinions with an absolute
certainty of their wrongness.")

Right at the start of the novel, Martin tells Helen, "[Y]ou
may look for beauty and find it in almost everything. . . . Father
finds it in the work of Demosthenes, but I in the works of Schumann." Benson here invokes Schumann as Forster does in *A
Room with a View*—as an example of a conflicted nature; when,
heated with passion, Martin tells his father, "[Y]ou must not
interfere with other people's individualities," we understand the
terms of his conflict (even though the novel fails to articulate
them).

The first of Martin's performances is of Chopin's first ballade.
Upon hearing it, Stella,

> who had been accustomed to consider the piano as an instru-
> ment for the encouragement of conversation after dinner, or at
> the most as the introduction to the vocal part of a concert,
> found herself sitting bolt upright in her chair with a strange tin-
> gling excitement spreading through her and a heightened and
> quickened beating of blood.

For Lady Sunningdale—an Ottoline Morrell type at whose house
Martin is playing—Chopin awakens a desire for something virtuosic, although the first ballade is certainly that. (Benson does
not tell how Martin became so expert a performer, this ballade

being beyond the means of any other kind of pianist.²) Obligingly, then, Martin launches into Brahms's *Paganini* variations. And just as in *A Room with a View* Lucy Honeychurch closes the piano when George enters the room at Windy Corner (when the piano is closed, Lucy is too), Martin closes the piano when his father enters the room and remarks, "And Martin wasting his time at the piano as usual." In the language of Schumann, Martin's father is a Philistine: his perception of music, to the extent that he may be said to possess one, is as weak as Stella's.

Later that night, while lying in his bed, Martin allows his mind to wander:

> [T]he exquisiteness of the sleeping summer night, peopled with ivory lights and ebony shadows, and the great velvet vault of the sky pricked by the thin remote fires of innumerable stars, and lit by that glorious sexless flame of the moon [*casta diva*], smote him with a sudden pang of pleasure. Somehow all this must be translatable into music.

In order to enable Martin to learn to "translate," then, Benson ere long produces a teacher for him in the person of Karl Rusoff. The boy plays Chopin's "fourth *étude*" (presumably opus 10, no. 4) and, again, the *Paganini* variations—performances impressive enough to convince Rusoff to accept Martin as a pupil. The lessons take place in Rusoff's house, which is described:

> The room itself was large, lofty and well-proportioned, and furnished with a certain costly simplicity. A few Persian rugs lay on the parquet floor, a French writing-table stood in the window, a tall bookcase glimmering with the gilt and morocco of fine bindings occupied nearly half of the wall in which the fireplace was set, two or three chairs formed a group with a sofa in the corner, and the Steinway grand occupied more than the area taken up by all the rest of the furniture. There perhaps simplicity gained its highest triumph; the case was of rosewood designed by Morris and the formal perfection of its lines was a thing only to be perceived by an artist. On the walls, finally, hung two or three prints, and on the mantelpiece were a

2. Similarly, Forster does not record the history of Lucy's piano lessons; nor does Forster's biographer, P. N. Furbank, know when and where Forster himself learned to play the piano.

couple of reproductions of Greek bronzes found at Hercula-
neum.

At the end, in a seeming throw-away line, Italy and what Italy
meant to the Victorian homosexual—a Mecca of available and
unpunishable sex—rears its glorious head. A few pages later, a
conversation between Martin and Rusoff makes fairly explicit
what Rusoff's decor has foretold. "Drink from every spring but
one, and drink deep," the old man tells his pupil, then paraphrases Pater (writing of William Morris): "To burn always with
this hard, gem-like flame, to maintain this ecstasy, is success in
life." But the spring is not, as Martin at first believes, (heterosexual) love.

> 'My God, if that had been granted to me,' [Rusoff] said, 'I too
> might have been great. But I never fell in love [with a woman].
> Oh! I am successful; I know, I understand. I am the only person
> perhaps who does know what is missing in me. It is that. But
> missing that, I never, no not once, parodied what I did not
> know. Parody, parody!' he repeated.

Martin intuits the sense of this masterpiece of the elliptical, and
answers, "I am not beastly. . . . I think you had no right to suppose that." Yet the mentor-pupil relationship between Rusoff and
Martin remains intact after Rusoff's confession because the subject of "beastliness" is—to use the word again—translated into a
general warning to Martin about the ways the world will try to
spoil him.

After that we hear no more on the dread subject of beastliness, for Benson abruptly has Martin declare himself to Stella.
(This is a favorite Benson device: in his first *Colin* novel, for example, Philip ups and marries, even though his life on Capri—
that island so beloved of Compton Mackenzie, the founder of
Gramophone magazine, Graham Greene and Norman Douglas
—seemed to be leading in an altogether different direction. In the
Mapp and Lucia series, even Georgino and Lucia marry, after all.)
Furthermore, so many are the wonders of heterosexual love that
shortly afterwards Martin gives his début playing a virtuoso program and achieves a success with it. Alas, however, he contracts
typhoid at that very moment, and so dies just as he approaches
his "musical" fruition.

The tragic early death of the artist is a romantic, if time-worn convention. In *The Challoners*, however, death is not the culmination of an artistic destiny: it is a failure. Benson lifted himself above outright hypocrisy (by not marrying Martin and Stella) yet lowered himself from the impressive heights of personal conviction (by not allowing Martin a long and music-filled life).

In Somerset Maugham's "The Alien Corn," the piano player is a boy named George, the scion of a Jewish family that has refashioned itself as a gentrified English one—having, in the process, taken the telling surname Bland. The ethnically divided nature of the family, like George's connection to the piano, encodes homosexuality here: George's parents have broken with his father's uncle, Ferdy Rabenstein, ostensibly because he would not change his name. Yet Ferdy himself is also a homosexual with all the trimmings.

> After dinner Ferdy was persuaded to play the piano. He only played Viennese waltzes, I discovered later that they were his specialty, and the light, tuneful and sensual music seemed to accord well with his discreet flamboyance. . . . His taste was perfect and many of his friends were glad to avail themselves of his knowledge. He was one of the first to value old furniture and he rescued many a priceless piece from the attics of ancestral mansions and gave it an honourable place in the drawing-room. It amused him to saunter round the auction rooms and he was always willing to give his advice to great ladies who desired at once to acquire a beautiful thing and make a profitable investment. He was rich and good-natured. He liked to patronize the arts and would take a great deal of trouble to get commissions for some young painter whose talent he admired or an engagement to play at a rich man's house for a violinist who could in no other way get a hearing.

In the event, Maugham writes (needlessly, of course) that Ferdy never married. "'I am a man of the world,' [Ferdy] said, ' . . . *tous les goûts sont dans la nature. . . .* '"

As for George: he, too, has no girlfriend. To be sure, music is his life. Although his father (like Martin's) does not esteem music, he finally assents to his son's wish to study in Munich. He grants him two years' support, at the end of which he will play for "some competent and disinterested person . . . and if then that person said he showed promise of becoming a first-rate pianist no further obstacles would be placed in his way." (George is not a virtuoso *sui generis*.) The "competent and disinterested person" who comes to hear George at the end of the allotted time is Lea Makart—a friend of Ferdy's, naturally—and what she hears him play is Chopin (two waltzes, a polonaise, and an *étude*). When George has finished auditioning, Makart tells him that "not in a thousand years" will he become a pianist of the first rank, and, before tea, plays the piano herself (music of J. S. Bach). The narrator, also a character in the story, becomes aware through Makart's playing of "a sturdy strength that seemed to have its roots deep in mother earth, and of an elemental power that was timeless and had no home in space." "That clinches it," George chuckles when she finishes, and on the next page he shoots himself.

In his last interview with his father, George tells him, "[T]he only thing in the world I want is to be a pianist. And there's nothing doing." Yet George *is* a pianist: a pianist is anyone who plays the piano—nothing more, nothing less. Moreover, Lea has also told him, "It will always be a pleasure to you to be able to play the piano and it will enable you to appreciate great playing as no ordinary person can hope to do." She has recognized that although George is not a virtuoso, he is not ordinary.

In life as in fiction, few people kill themselves because they cannot play a musical instrument well enough.[3] In Isherwood's "On Ruegen Island (Summer 1931)," for instance, Peter (also homosexual) goes to Paris to study music, and supports himself with a legacy from an uncle, since his father has disenfranchised him. "His teacher told him that he would never be more than a good second-rate amateur," Isherwood writes, "but he only worked all the harder. He worked merely to avoid thinking, and had another nervous breakdown, less serious than at first."

---

3. Wertheimer, a character in Thomas Bernhard's *The Loser*, hangs himself because he cannot surpass the playing of Glenn Gould, whom he met in Salzburg twenty-eight years before, when they both studied with Horowitz. It is Gould who calls Wertheimer "the loser."

The first work of fiction in English to illustrate expressly a connection between music and homosexuality—by the turn of the century, "musical" was an accepted euphemism for homosexual—is Edward Prime-Stevenson's *Imre: A Memorandum* (1906). Having vehemently voiced his personal terror and disgust of "those types of men-loving-men who, by thousands, live incapable of any noble ideals or lives" and named "sugary and fibreless" musicians among the ignobles, the narrator nonetheless admits that music formed "the very tissue of intimacy, of life, with *him* [Imre]." When the narrator believes that he has lost Imre, his feeling for music is transformed into "a dull hatred, . . . a detestation, a contempt, a horror!" for the "super-neurotic, quintessentially sexual, perniciously homosexual art—mystery—that music is!"[4]

In his determination to portray an ideal of romantic friendship between men, Prime-Stevenson keeps *Imre* scrupulously clean of sex; indeed, a recent paperback edition of the novel contains *interpolated* pornographic scenes. In this regard *Imre* provides a sharp contrast to a curious sub-genre of literature about *virtuosi* that concerns itself with the (homo)sexual virtuoso— of whom Teleny, the eponymous hero of an unsigned Victorian novel, is the paragon.

---

4. A still earlier work illustrating the connection between music and a neurotic, hyperaesthetic disposition is Huysmans's *Against the Grain* (1884). From chapter 15:

> Certain settings for the violoncello by Schumann had left him positively panting with emotion, gasping for breath under the stress of hysteria; but it was chiefly Schubert's *lieder* that had stirred him to the depths, lifted him out of himself, then prostrated him as after a wasteful outpouring of nervous fluid, after a mystic debauch of soul.

The subject of homosexuality is presented in volume two of Rolland's *Jean-Christophe*, wherein the romantic friendship between the eponymous hero and a youth named Otto is, in time, subjected to "certain sarcastic allusions," "the unwholesome curiosity of the town," and so on. Rolland does not actually give cause for such an interpretation of the boys' friendship in the novel, so it is curious that he should elect to have other of his characters see it in that light.

9.
The Virtuoso at Home

Teleny, published anonymously in 1893, tells the story of a young Hungarian virtuoso pianist (possibly a tribute to the memory of Liszt, who had been dead only seven years) and his lover, Des Grieux (also the name of Manon's lover). Although compelling in its own right, *Teleny* has gained in literary interest over the years as a consequence of its link to Oscar Wilde—the most illustrious of those candidates put forward for its authorship. (Beardsley contributed to the body of Victorian pornography with his *Under the Hill*; so, too, did Swinburne with his *Whippingham Papers*.) Of course, whether Wilde ultimately penned *Teleny*, or even part of it, is of little consequence—the novel would be neither better nor worse for this knowledge—but playing detective is irresistible.

To wit: Wilde was almost the only important writer of the time, in English, in whose works men—Algernon Moncrieff (*The Importance of Being Earnest*) and Dorian Gray, to name but two—commonly play the piano; his poem "In the Gold Room: A Harmony," with its female pianist, being something of an anomaly in his *oeuvre*. Moncrieff and Gray, of course, are avowed amateurs, whereas Teleny is a full-fledged virtuoso.[1] Here is the scene in which Des Grieux first hears Teleny, who is playing a "wild Hungarian rhapsody":

> That thrilling longing I had felt grew more and more intense, the craving so insatiable that it was changed to pain; the

---

1. George Eliot had met and become friendly with Liszt while sojourning in Weimar with George Henry Lewes during the late summer and autumn of 1854. As a result, the first great male virtuoso pianist in literature, in English, might well be Klesmer in *Daniel Deronda*, Eliot's last novel.

> burning fire had now been fanned into a mighty flame, and
> my whole body was convulsed and writhed with mad desire.
> My lips were parched, I gasped for breath; my joints were stiff,
> my veins were swollen, yet I sat still, like all the crowd around
> me. But suddenly a heavy hand seemed to be laid upon my lap,
> something was hent and clasped and grasped, which made me
> faint with lust. The hand moved up and down, slowly at first,
> then fast and faster it went in rhythm with the song. My brain
> began to reel as throughout every vein a burning lava coursed,
> and then, some drops even gushed out—I panted—

Thus, *Teleny* emphasizes another mystic aspect of the virtuoso:
the sexual nature, always at least partially explicit, of his achievement. In his memoir *Cannons and Flowers*, the Hungarian virtuoso
Cziffra describes an encounter with a "strange fellow" in Budapest in the 1940s. When the fellow asks him, "Can you improvise
on absolutely anything?" Cziffra nods.

> 'Even in the dark?' he went on, lowering his voice. 'What
> dark?,' I asked, astonished. 'Pitch dark, my dear fellow,' he
> whispered mysteriously. 'A very intimate cabaret frequented
> by regulars and important persons who wish to remain incog-
> nito. It has just re-opened in the city centre.' As he observed my
> reactions, he started using jargon: 'We need a pianist who can
> cope with anything. He must do psychadelic [*sic*] improvisa-
> tions to create an . . . shall we say "aphrodisiac" tension to pro-
> voke passion in hypersensitive people, not to speak of special
> types of friendship.'

In short, the strange fellow is looking for a virtuoso. (Cziffra's an-
ecdote suggests the existence of a homosexual underground in
Budapest with which Teleny, too, might have been familiar.)

But to return to Wilde: the suite of Teleny's rooms described
in the passages excerpted below gives more than a passing nod
to rooms in Wilde's own house in London's Tite Street (no. 16).
There was a white room there, but it was the dining room rather
than the bedroom. The bathroom, however, was also lit by a skylight, while the décor of the smoking room was North African.

In *Teleny*, the rooms in which the virtuoso lives (and the uses
to which he puts them) tell much about his personality. Near
the beginning of the novel, for instance, Teleny and Des Grieux
fuck in

a most peculiar room, the walls of which were covered over with some warm, white, soft, quilted stuff, studded all over with frosted silver buttons; the floor was covered with the curly white fleece of young lambs; in the middle of the apartment stood a capacious couch, on which was thrown the skin of a huge polar bear. Over this single piece of furniture, an old silver lamp—evidently from some Byzantine church or some Eastern synagogue—shed a pale glimmering light, sufficient, however, to light up the dazzling whiteness of this temple of Priapus whose votaries we were.

The lovers then repair their toilet in "a kind of cell, all filled with ferns and feathery palms, that—as [Teleny] shewed me—received during the day the rays of the sun from a skylight overhead." Finally, they take dinner and smoke in "a neighbouring room all covered with thick, soft, and silky carpets, the prevailing tone of which was dull Turkish red."

> In the center of this apartment hung a curiously-wrought, starshaped lamp, which the faithful—even now-a-days—light on Friday eve.
> We sat down on a soft-cushioned divan, in front of one of those ebony Arab tables all inlaid with coloured ivory and iridescent mother-of-pearl.

In sum, whether Wilde is describing his own rooms, or whether they are being described by someone else, room description in the novel provides a means of evoking both the glamour and the erotic power of the virtuoso; it also provides the paradigm for descriptions of the homosexual virtuoso's house that find their echo in a host of later books about pianists.

* * *

Liberace (né Wladziu Valentino Liberace, in 1919) wrote, in collaboration with Carol Truax—in her own right the author of such titles as *Father was a Gourmet* and *The Art of Salad Making*—a bestselling cookbook. It was published as *Liberace Cooks!* although Liberace had wanted it to be entitled *Mother, I'd Rather Do It Myself!* The gimmick of this project is that each of the "hundreds of delicious recipes" comes from one of the *seven* dining rooms in the entertainer's Hollywood house. (He had another in Palm

Springs, yet another in Spain with a view of the Rock of Gibral-
tar.) And in the same way that seven veils reveal the Princess
Salome, these seven dining rooms reveal Liberace near the apex
of his fame.

In the event, Truax tries her best to negate what David Berg-
man calls "The Liberace Effect" (that is, "to be so exaggerated an
example of what you in fact are that people think you couldn't
possibly be it") by emphasizing the pianist's masculinity. Her description of his "strong Roman emperor features," however, is entirely subverted by such priceless text as, "It's the sauces that di-
vide the men from the boys" (from chapter eight, "Sauces, Sauces
Everywhere") or "Wise in the ways of appetite, Liberace exploits
the art of broiling. Not only steaks and chops get cooked over
glowing coals, his kebabs are a conversation piece. . . ." (from
chapter five, "Cookout on the Loggia"). Her descriptions of Liberace's decor are equally subversive. The ground level of his
house, for example, "planned for performances and performance
parties," features

> A large salon furnished with comfortable couches in red bro-
> cade velvet, set off by accents of black Chinese lacquer and gold
> trim. The biggest item in lacquer is a huge Chinese cabinet,
> with three sections of five shelves each, crowded with minia-
> ture pianos. . . .

The formal dining room—the epitome of his aspirations—is also
"a large salon," but this time decorated in a white and gold color
scheme.

> The deep pile carpet is cream, and the brocade on the walls is
> white on white. Against the walls there are long buffets, and
> glass-fronted cabinets full of silver and cut glass. A long oval
> table seats twelve. The chairs are French blond picked out with
> gilding, with woven cane backs. Overhead is a splendid crystal
> chandelier with twenty-four lights. The table is covered with a
> fabulous lace cloth, hand crocheted of gold bullion thread and
> adorned with pear-shaped cut crystal drops around the edge.
> The table service gleams with red and gold, and so does the
> pair of many branching candelabra.

The purpose of these descriptions is no doubt to suggest the
"elegance" and "luxury" of Liberace's house—an excess in keep-

ing with the excess of his "talent." In any case, they confirm the complete lack of refinement in everything that "Mr. Showmanship" touched: his houses were as gaudy and tawdry as his piano playing. (The house presents a remarkable contrast to Elvis Presley's Memphis house, Graceland: though lacking in "good taste," Graceland makes no pretenses.)

Truax's homosexual intonation is also found, unexpectedly, in Abram Chasins's description of the "bachelor quarters" of Van Cliburn in *The Van Cliburn Legend:*

> One-third of his pale gray living room was taken up by his inseparable companion—the graceful, big Steinway. An entire wall was dominated by an in-a-bed sofa, in case his parents should come up for a visit. But the chairs, tables, dressers, lamps . . . all reflected the personal taste he now was developing.
>
> Between concerts he went to museums and galleries and fascinating shops. At the museum of the Frick Collection, soon a favorite haunt, he discovered a natural affinity for the romantic elegance of the great French periods. Most of the pieces he picked up in the auction rooms were either Louis XVI or Empire, and some of his acquisitions were frankly bargains. Everything showed fine discrimination—a fruit-wood bureau with large, brass handles; a Directoire bench for the long narrow hallway, where Hogarth prints embellished the wall; a low, marble-topped table. Antique mirrors, stacked against the fireplace, blocked out the garish hardness of painted red brick. But Chinese red was used from floor to ceiling in the tiny kitchenette, to suggest the inside of a bright, lacquered box.

When, later, we read that Cliburn also acquired "a fine Sheraton secretary and a richly covered *bergere* [*sic*]," it is hard not to hear the subversive message in Chasins's characterization of Cliburn as a "born flaming virtuoso." Irving Kolodin, reviewing Cliburn's 1958 performance of Rachmaninov's third with the New York Philharmonic, called it an outright "feminine one":

> . . . incisive attacks were being reduced to pin points of emphasis, while strongly affirmative statements of deep feeling were being downgraded to rather supine curves of sentimentality. A lack of tonal mass to override the orchestra at crucial moments in the first and final movements was another limiting factor,

plus an inclination to indulge the weaker aspects of the composer's creation at cost to the stronger.

(In the early 1990s, John Browning, Cliburn's chief rival, was
interviewed for the *New York Times* by Barbara Jepson. Although
she described his house simply as an "eclectically furnished
34th-floor apartment on the Upper East Side of Manhattan," she
took pains to note—and Virgil Thomson could not have done so
better—that the pianist had "just returned from his waterfront
home in northern Wisconsin, which he shares with Tyler, a Papillon show dog." Her language is wicked and careful: "shares" sets
up an expectation in the Fosterian sense (that the pianist "shares"
with a "friend"), while the reference not simply to a dog, but to "a
Papillon show dog," hints at a distinct lack of butchness. (Mozart
and Poulenc, like me, were fox-terrier men.) To bring her point
home, Jepson goes on to write of the pianist: "[He] has remarkable genes or dyes his hair brown. . . ." The miracle on the 34th
floor is that Browning did not push Jepson out of the window.)

From a profile of Bolet published in the *Australian Women's
Weekly*, we learn that

> Bolet, a bachelor . . . believes that every musical performance
> should have what he calls "color and texture." . . . "[T]he walls
> of my home are plastered with colorful paintings. Dull, somber
> paintings don't say enough for me. . . . Color is a personal thing
> in your home. I have so much color on the walls I have to keep
> plain upholstery like black leather and subdued shades of
> blues and greens, with perhaps an occasional pair of mustard
> colored chairs. I would love to have a sofa with a big, bold pat-
> tern, but I can't." . . . Gorgeous is a favorite word he likes a lot.
> He described the barrier reef as "Gorgeous."

To understand that decoration may encode sexuality, one
need only compare Cliburn's and Bolet's digs with those of the
known heterosexual Pollini (whose son Daniele, incidentally, is
also a pianist[2]). David Mellor describes his Milan apartment as
"like the man himself, stylish, cool and elegant":

2. Pollini *fils* played this super-virtuoso program in Florence, at the Teatro
della Pergola, on 28 March 1999: Stockhausen's *Klavierstück V,* Scriabin's *Vers la
flamme,* Ravel's *Gaspard,* Stockhausen's *Klavierstück IX,* Ravel's *Miroirs,* and Debussy's *L'Isle joyeuse.*

The walls are white, the furniture modern, sparse but comfortable, and the whole is pleasingly minimalist in effect. Books on art and philosophy jostle for attention with beautiful abstract sculptures and paintings, predominantly the work of Pollini's uncle, a distinguished artist who enjoyed considerable success in the 1930s and 1940s.

That the description of decor can be uninflected, and ignore the sexuality of its occupant, is demonstrated by Samuel Chotzinoff's survey of Horowitz's living room on Manhattan's East 94th Street—a house he bought from the playwright George S. Kauffmann:

At the end of the Horowitzes' living room two concert grands stand side by side. . . . On the walls hang four masterpieces of painting. One is a painting of Madame Manet by her husband, Édouard Manet. . . . The others are a pastel by Degas of jockeys on their mounts, a head of a girl by Rouault and, perhaps the cream of the collection, Picasso's *Acrobat en Repos.*

10.
Possibilities of a Homosexual Aesthetic of Virtuosity

In 1990, Susan McClary delivered a now rather (in)famous, if actually modest, paper on Schubert for the first panel on gay issues at the American Musicological Society: "Constructions of Subjectivity in Schubert's Music." After she presented this same paper at the "Schubertiade" of the 92nd Street Y in New York two years later, both Edward Rothstein and Bernard Holland went after her in the pages of *The New York Times* for daring to ask "whether or not [Schubert's] music responded in any way to his sexual orientation" and "*on the basis of the music itself* whether Schubert was gay." McClary describes the *Times*'s treatment of her paper in a "Prelude" appended to it prior to its publication in *Queering the Pitch: The New Gay and Lesbian Musicology*.

> Working from an early draft the staff at the Y happened to have had on hand, Edward Rothstein reported on the event as a whole, with a somewhat skeptical account of my contribution. . . . Two weeks later, Rothstein's column in the Sunday edition of the *Times* presented a more antagonistic treatment of my arguments, followed the next day with a smug parody by his colleague Bernard Holland.
>
> Still operating under the illusion that the New York establishment was basically liberal, I wrote a reply, as did Philip Brett and Elizabeth Wood. We waited. Every Sunday I dutifully bought the *Times* to see our letters. Nothing. Finally some phone calls confirmed that the *New York* ("All the News That's Fit to Print") *Times* had not seen fit to print our answers.

Indirectly, McClary got it again from the *Times* in James B. Oestreich's review of Brian Newbould's *Schubert: The Music and the Man.* "What is not known, like the nature of Schubert's sexual orientation, which has attracted so much speculation of late," he coos approvingly, "detains [Newbould] little." Then, as if to put paid once and for all to the whole distasteful notion of a homosexual Schubert, Oestreich quotes the biographer himself:

> Since no one has yet demonstrated that there is an identifiable gay way of proportioning a sonata movement, structuring a cadence, arguing a fugue or handling a symphony orchestra, the question of sexuality would seem to have little bearing on our consideration of Schubert's music.

What is so troubling about the *Times*'s response to McClary is its admixture of defensiveness and smugness; also the ruthlessness with which the provoking work is rejected rather than used as a basis for the fair and serious assessment, or reassessment, of feelings and values. (Karl Hugo Pruys caused a similar "outrage" in Germany when he proposed, in *Die Liebkosungen des Tigrers,* that Goethe was homosexual.) Indeed, the real problem here is less the denunciation of homosexuality than the crude imposition of heterosexuality in its place, even when no positive evidence can be found to justify that imposition. In other words, it is not enough to say, "Schubert was not homosexual." One must say, "Schubert was not homosexual, he was heterosexual." Yet, might not the composer have been bisexual? (No one has as yet taken a "queer theory" look at Charles Henri de Blainville's discovery, in the eighteenth century, of a mode between major and minor, which is rather like Edward Carpenter's "Intermediate Sex.") When irrefutable documentary evidence establishes a composer's (or interpreter's) homosexuality, one rejoices because, at the very least, such evidence takes the wind out of the bigot's sails. There are, however, forces which militate even against such documentary evidence. Thus, though Chopin's letters to Tytus Woychiechowski are explicitly homoerotic, Arthur Hedley's edition of Chopin's letters purges them of all such feeling. (Sydow's three-volume French edition is more reliable.)

I must acknowledge that possibly I am entering the lion's den to write of homosexuality and music together, given that no one yet has been able to marry these subjects in a manner that rubs neither heterosexuals nor homosexuals—terms of inescapable tyranny—the wrong way. Indeed, the reception of both McClary's work and Maynard Solomon's investigations into Schubert's homosexuality ("Franz Schubert's 'My Dream'" and "Franz Schubert and the Peacocks of Benvenuto Cellini") show that critics do take issue with the "homosexualization" of their musical idols— as if adoration of the homosexual implicates. Homosexuals are no less vocal in their reactions to so-called "gay studies"—either because of deep feelings against the squandered opportunities represented by books published in the field or because of internalized homophobia. (Wayne Koestenbaum's *The Queen's Throat* and Kevin Kopelson's *Beethoven's Kiss*, for example, are not so much about music as about their authors' obsessions: in the first case with divas, in the second with Wayne Koestenbaum.)

Having disburdened myself, then, of this account of the perils inherent in writing about the subject, I would like to focus on the homosexual aesthetic of performance. Let me begin by deploring the clichés upon which McClary bases her analysis of Schubert's B minor symphony; that is, having a "weak," or homosexual, theme crushed by a more powerful heterosexual one. Why must the homosexual theme be the weaker one? (The most astute and profitable writing on music and sexuality I have read is Kallberg's *Chopin at the Boundaries*.) McClary missed an opportunity to assert the audacious *privilege* of being homosexual because she is as ideological, as homophobic and, ultimately, as sanctimonious as (some of) her critics, unable to treat of Schubert as anything other than a prop in a heterosexual and phallocentric drama. For example, her assertion that the homosexual composer eschews "goal-oriented desire *per se* for the sake of a sustained image of pleasure and an open, flexible sense of self" diminishes individual experience through the repetition of emasculating, if ostensibly "positive," clichés.

In the end, musical *performance*—specifically, virtuoso performance—may provide a better way into exploring the presence or absence of homosexual elements in music. Here, one can propose the possibility of a homosexual aesthetic of interpretation even as one fully admits that parallel aesthetics exist and must also be considered. Is there, for example, a comparable hetero-sexual, or lesbian, or overlapping homosexual-heterosexual style of *interpretation*? Theory becomes dangerous when it sets limits instead of crossing borders.

What might distinguish a virtuoso homosexual aesthetic of interpretation is an insistence chiefly upon a sense of beauty and style. *Carnaval* is not Schumann's best music, but the way Ego-rov played it, no one would believe that it was not: his perform-ance of Schumann's portrait of "Chopin" could bring tears from a stone because beautiful sound was integral to his Romantic—and virtuoso—playing. (Egorov's playing of "Chopin" observed, almost uniquely, Schumann's *agitato* and *forte* indications—indications which are important because they convey Schu-mann's understanding of Chopin's music: inquietude beneath beauty.) Neuhaus regarded tone as "the substance of music" and its mastery as the first of all problems of technique. This concep-tion of tone is integral to a proper understanding of virtuosity in the larger sense: not as an end in itself, but as a means to an end; as Neuhaus writes in *The Art of Piano Playing*, "The concept of beauty of tone is not sensuously static but dialectic; the best tone, consequently the most beautiful, is the one which renders a par-ticular meaning in the best possible manner." Brendel and Lupu sometimes play, on the contrary, with little regard for beautiful tone—even in music in which beauty itself (yet not *only* beauty of tone) *is* a meaning. In the case of Lupu, this is perplexing: he was a Neuhaus pupil, and possibly on this basis is reputed, by those who have not heard him in concert, "never to have pro-duced an ugly sound in his life." Anyone who has heard him in concert, however, knows this to be untrue. Gould was even less in-clined to produce beautiful tone (and recorded no work of Schu-mann's for solo piano): the revelation of structure was his musical grail. (How odd, then, that he neglected Godowsky's work.) Yet structural concerns do not preclude the wooing of beauty. (That beautiful tone alarmed Gould is suggested by his feelings of em-barrassment and offense when Bernstein once praised his playing with the admission, "I almost came in my pants.")

To be sure, Schumann's music is a litmus test for virtuoso playing; not only is it technically harrowing, its eloquent crazi-ness, its boisterousness and diffidence and painful delicacy, is very difficult to capture. (Géza Anda did so.) A Platonic ideal of beauty remains an inherent part of Romantic music, even as the conception of what is beautiful changes with epochs. And for the homosexual, the idea of a beauty that answers only to itself may be part of a larger effort to ennoble an embattled form of love.

A homosexual aesthetic is not evident exclusively in *how* a pianist plays, however: it is also evident in *what* a pianist plays. Stephen Hough, for example, has made a laudable specialty not only of rescuing works that have fallen into neglect and obscurity, but also of premiering and recording works by a number of homosexual composers (John Corigliano and Lowell Liebermann, for example) and transcribing in the virtuoso tradition. He included his own versions of two songs by the homosexual English composer Roger Quilter as well as "My Favorite Things" from Rodgers and Hammerstein's 1959 musical *The Sound of Music* on his first CD of virtuoso pieces, while on his second he offered another Quilter transcription and another Rodgers and Hammerstein arrangement: "March of the Siamese Children" from *The King and I.* (His third piano album includes yet more transcriptions of Rogers's music: "Hello Young Lovers" and "Carousel Waltz.") Is anything more "gay" than the American musical theater? Similarly, Wild transcribed five songs from Walt Disney's *Snow White and the Seven Dwarfs,* quoting coyly from "Someday My Prince Will Come" (practically a homosexual anthem), while Pletnev transcribed (and has recorded) suites from Tchaikovsky's ballets *The Nutcracker* and *The Sleeping Beauty* stunningly. All of these transcriptions are a kind of Camp, and as Sontag explained in her essay "Notes on 'Camp'" (1964), "while it's not true that Camp taste *is* homosexual taste, there is no doubt a peculiar affinity and overlap. . . . homosexuals, by and large, constitute the vanguard—and the most articulate audience—of Camp." Homosexuals also recognize most easily the truth and integrity of sincere experience that swathes itself in Camp.

Finally, it does seem that in music homosexual men are rarely "size queens." In general, it is heterosexuals who want to play the big sonatas, the big concerti; who are driven to prove themselves strong, virile, potent, heroically hung. Perahia, who played first in Florence during an incredible week when Richter and Pollini also came to town, performed for nearly two and a half hours—

as if, for him, Florence was a sort of locker room in which he wanted to prove that his musical penis was grander, or that his staying power was greater, than that of either of his colleagues. For though Perahia has plenty of technique, he has lost his ability to sing. On the other hand, homosexual virtuosi have traditionally shown an uncanny affinity for the smaller works that Joseph Horowitz, in an article on Vladimir Horowitz, dismissed contemptuously as "brains-in-the-fingers cameos." That critic's bias is apparent even in his choice of metaphor. (The fact that heterosexual virtuosi often have their performances described as "granitic" and so on is a notable counterpoint to the descriptions that the playing of homosexuals—and women—often evoke: runs like pearls, textures like gossamer. . . .)

When Clara Schumann sojourned in Florence many years after her husband's death, Elizabeth von Herzogenberg wrote to Brahms that the city's beauty made Clara nervous:

> we found her sitting on her stool before a Signorelli or a Verocchio looking very worried, rubbing her hands in fearful enthusiasm—she would not let herself be emotionally carried away or allow her soul, so capable of vibration, to stir.

Even Goethe had been afraid of Florence. In his *Italian Journey,* he wrote (on 25 October 1786):

> I took a quick walk through the city to see the Duomo and the Battistero. Once more, a completely new world opened up before me, but I did not wish to stay long. . . . I hurried out of the city as quickly as I entered it.

11.

Celluloid

In the 1960s, RCA executives went to Horowitz, who was then recording under the eye of the ever-faithful fox terrier Nipper, and asked him if he would record works along the lines of Rossini's *William Tell* and Tchaikovsky's *1812* overtures rather than more Clementi sonatas and Scriabin arcana: they were hoping for a commercial, rather than a critical, success from him. Shortly thereafter, Horowitz went over to Columbia, where he made some of his finest records—among them *Horowitz Plays Scarlatti*, his May 1965 concert at Carnegie Hall, and his first *Kreisleriana*.

Ultimately, the pianist who midwifed the sort of works RCA asked Horowitz to record was Liberace. In a grotesque parody of the virtuoso's catholicity of taste, he was as at home playing Schubert's "Ave Maria" (not in Liszt's transcription, of course) as the "Beer Barrel Polka" and "Somewhere My Love" (from the film *Doctor Zhivago*).

Liberace had studied the piano more or less seriously and claimed even to have received the praise of Paderewski. A key piece of evidence suggests that Liberace knew little about Paderewski except that he was a famous pianist. Liberace said that after he met Paderewski, the great pianist returned "to his castle in Budapest." (Paderewski actually lived in Riond Bosson, Switzerland.) What is significant, in any case, is the importance of Paderewski's praise to Liberace's myth of himself; reminiscent of the "kiss of consecration" Liszt received from Beethoven. For although Liberace did play Liszt's A major concerto with Frederick Stock and the Chicago Symphony Orchestra, in Milwaukee, in 1939, in the end his sensibilities simply did not dispose him to classical music: he found in New York and Las Vegas the true country of his soul.

> . . . then along came television, and pretty soon I was playing for a million listeners, and they all liked me. They liked my classical piano, and the jokes I couldn't help making. They liked the Chopin candelabra lighting the piano, and pretty soon they liked the unusual turnouts I began to wear. I knew that they also liked the warm, essentially modest, Liberace whom they glimpsed beneath the glittering facade.

Liszt's most brilliant period of performance was called his *Glanzzeit*. No one had ever before played the piano as he did, and so this period of "glitter"—"brilliant" in the French or Italian sense of diamond-like rather than the Anglo-Saxon sense of supremely intelligent—had a grand purpose. (When Cardus wrote in "The Genius of Liszt" that the composer seemed "to foretell the advent of Hollywood in a splash of limelight grandiloquence; he gives us 'fade-outs,' cavalcades, purple and goldleaf," he was evoking the works of the *Glanzzeit*.) Liberace looked back to Liszt's "glitter"—a "rhinestone Rubinstein" was but one of the many sobriquets (repeatable in polite society) by which he was known—even as he *pavéed* the way for popular musicians like Elton John and the more sartorially sober (but classically trained) Victor Borge. For him, though, there was *only* the glitter. As his aggressively deceitful and self-congratulatory autobiography makes all too clear, there was no musical and moral iron beneath it, which did not stop him from becoming for millions of people (mostly middle-aged and old ladies) the embodiment of the (lowest) popular idea of the virtuoso. In this regard he emulated the phenomenon of Paderewski, who was, as Sorabji put it, "the man-in-the-street's beau-idéal of a world-famous pianist."

The Liberace phenomenon in miniature was shown in the 1955 film *Sincerely Yours*, in which he himself played a pianist named Anthony Warrin whose dream is to give a classical concert in Carnegie Hall. After any number of riotous episodes—Liberace as a heterosexual romantic lead, acts of altruism springing from acts of voyeurism (thanks to lip-reading lessons and a pair of powerful binoculars)—Warrin finally acquits himself of

Tchaikovsky's first concerto in that hallowed auditorium. He cannot live by Tchaikovsky alone, however, so by way of an encore he plays "When Irish Eyes Are Smiling" for friends in the audience. Then, by way of another encore, equally full of blarney, he plays what I believe is the Notre Dame fight song for a formerly crippled boy who, having regained the use of his legs thanks to an operation paid for by Warrin, hopes to play football. As Warrin plays, not only the many friends he has made during the course of the film (among them a woman whose uppity daughter has kept her hidden from the socially superior in-laws), but indeed all the members of the audience, sing along. Backstage, the director of Carnegie Hall tells Liberace's manager that he has never heard anything like it. (I believe it.)

Anthony Warrin is the ambassador from the Land of Folksy Pretensions to the Court of Serious Culture: all those stuffy, bejeweled, and beminked society ladies and their tuxedoed husbands are much happier with the old tunes he plays—more famous than even the big opening theme of the Tchaikovsky first concerto. It is a very uncomfortable scene to watch, for in it virtuosity is discounted, made shameful, shamful; no longer is it, as James might have said, "the distinguished thing."

There was no irony in *Sincerely Yours;* nor, for that matter, was there much in the way of sincerity—musical or otherwise. Liberace was an arrogant, cynical man. He might have cried all the way to the bank, as he famously claimed, but he was spiritually and artistically bankrupt. His life, like his death, was notable for its indifference toward the common good, so that he could play in Apartheid South Africa with the justification: "If I'm invited to a man's home do I criticize his life style?" (Possibly he was operating on the principle, "People who play glass pianos should never throw stones.") Not only did he never accept his own homosexuality (which was not uncommon for a man of his generation), he went to inordinate pains to prove that he was *not* homosexual—even when he was dying of AIDS and the object of a sordid palimony suit initiated by his former lover and on-stage chauffeur, Scott Thorsen. Earlier in his life, he had brought a libel suit against a columnist from London's *Daily Mirror,* William Neil Connor, who wrote under what Liberace called the *nom de slur* of Cassandra, because Connor had suggested in print that Liberace was what Nicolas Slonimsky once unforgettably termed "a practitioner of the inverted mode of love." (Cassandra considered Liberace "the summit of sex. . . . Everything that He, She and It can ever want.") Unbelievably, Liberace won both this case and another against Jimmy Thompson, a comedian whose impression of him he learned about during the course of the Cassandra trial. Thompson's impression featured both a wig and a song with the verse "My fan mail is simply tremendous / It's growing so fast my head whirls, I get more and more / They propose by the score / And at least one or two are from girls." The last chapter of his autobiography is a list of his "girlfriends," among them the Norwegian figure skater and actress Sonja Henie; a pathetic version of Leporello's "catalogue" aria in *Don Giovanni*.

* * *

The unlikely sequel to *Sincerely Yours*—and indeed to the Liberace Phenomenon—is the story of the dreadful Australian pianist David Helfgott, told in the film *Shine*. The plots of the two films dovetail insofar as both Warrin and Helfgott make comebacks from debilitating circumstances; the former from deafness, the latter from mental collapse. As it happens, the scene in which Helfgott falls apart—playing the Rachmaninov third, mythologized in the film to the point that one would think no one had ever managed to play it before (no fewer than ninety pianists have recorded it[1])—is practically the same as the one in which Warrin loses his hearing while playing Chopin's A-flat major polonaise. That the onset of Warrin's deafness and Helfgott's actual collapse both come while they are in the throes of performing allows for some hokey effects: instead of hearing music, Warrin hears nothing; Helfgott, the beating of his own heart.[2]

Obeying the time-honored Hollywood tradition, each pianist falls in love at the end of his respective film; an occurrence that is slightly unprepared for in *Shine* as a consequence of an elliptical

1. The concerto was never played by its dedicatee: Josef Hofmann.
2. The plot device of the deaf pianist is also employed, less mawkishly if more drearily, in Vikram Seth's novel *An Equal Music*, which traces the love affair between a violinist in a string quartet and a pianist who has essentially lost her hearing.

scene involving Helfgott and a man in drag during the former's student days at the Royal College of Music in London. (Warrin's "woman" is the secretary who has long carried a torch for him, while Helfgott's is an erstwhile astrologer and "esoteric lecturer," his senior by more than fifteen years.) Thus bolstered by Venus, each man comes out the other side—Warrin after a tricky surgery, Helfgott after institutionalization—to play with new joy for Everyman. (In Helfgott's case, though, the "other side" is dark, since the cost of his present celebrity is the ransacking of his "story.")

In any event, Helfgott's story is not unique. Oscar Levant was also more famous for his mental illness than for his playing. An enormously popular television personality who starred in such films as *Humoresque, Rhapsody in Blue* (about his friend George Gershwin), and *An American in Paris,* Levant appeared frequently on celebrity panel shows, where he would often crack jokes about his drug addictions and shock treatments. Likewise the inherited schizophrenia of John Ogdon was chronicled not only in *Virtuoso* —a book written by his wife, pianist Brenda Lucas, and Michael Kerr—but also in a television film starring Alfred Molina and Alison Steadman. (Ogdon died, a suicide, at the age of 52.)

Similarities of plot are not the only correspondences between *Sincerely Yours* and *Shine,* however: the movies have the same fake atmosphere—although *Shine* is certainly better acted—and the same flaw: stories about indomitable artists are fine and good, but an artist's values and accomplishments (or lack of same) cannot be dismissed so lightly as they are here. In the end, neither Warrin's nor Helfgott's story is worthy of telling when held up against the untold stories of truer artists. Where, after all, is the movie about Lipatti's leukemia? About Solomon's stroke, or Delius's syphilis, or Ravel's aphasia? About Kathleen Ferrier's cancer, or Cyril Smith's thrombosis, which paralyzed his left arm, and to which he responded creatively by playing duets for three hands—as before the accident he had played four-hand repertoire—with his wife, pianist Phyllis Sellick? Those familiar with *Sincerely Yours* and other films of its ilk recognize the indiscriminate banality of *Shine:* it is as fake-true as Liberace's "virtuosity."

Some years ago Merchant-Ivory decided to produce a movie about the life of Nyiregyházi, concentrating on his remarkable "comeback" in the early 1970s and subsequent re-retreat into obscurity. With the success of *Shine*, however, the company— fearing that the public would not accept a second film about a pianist emerging from obscurity—scrapped the project. Once again, kitsch won out.

The most notable precedent for the film about a musician is Abel Gance's *Beethoven* (1936),[3] which gave rise to a flood of Holly- wood bio-pics: *A Song to Remember* (a Chopin story from 1944), *Song of Love* (a Schumann story from 1947, in one scene of which Brahms and Schumann each try to get out of killing a chicken for a New Year's dinner party), *Song without End* (a Liszt story from 1960), and *Amadeus* (a Mozart story from 1984). As historical doc- uments the majority of these are of scant worth (although as pure entertainment some of them can be quite extraordinary). *A Song to Remember*, however, is anomalous—among Hollywood's inter- pretations of composers lives in general, and among interpreta- tions of Chopin's specifically—insofar as it succeeded, by acci- dent, in doing Chopin a real service.

That Chopin was an ardent patriot is well known, and, suit- ably, his patriotism is the aspect of the composer's life empha- sized by the film. After a childhood and early manhood spent in his native Poland, Chopin, played by Cornel Wilde, goes to Paris with his teacher, Joseph Elsner, played by Paul Muni. There, in the salon of Pleyel, he meets Liszt, and they play together Cho- pin's *Heroic* polonaise—even though, in reality, it had not yet been written: Chopin reached Paris in 1831, and composed this work in 1842. In the film the famous polonaise simply provides an oc- casion for the two virtuosi to "meet cute," as they say in Holly- wood: Liszt does not want to stop playing the marvelous new work in order to shake Chopin's hand, but Chopin figures out that they can shake after all if, on their respective pianos, Liszt plays the right hand part of the polonaise while he himself plays

3. Gance's was not the first film about Beethoven, however. Another, in which the role of Beethoven was played by F. Kortner, was shown at the Théâtre du Trocadéro, Paris, on 6 April 1927, on the occasion of the centenary of the com- poser's death. While no copy of this film appears to have survived, I turned up a packet of fifteen cards picturing scenes from it from a *bouquiniste* on the Quai du Louvre.

the left. They do this with a *bonhomie* reminiscent of the protagonists of the Three Tenors concerts.

Not long afterwards—and also without much in the way of historical precedent—George Sand (played by Merle Oberon) co-opts Chopin and begins to dominate him. She is very happy when both the man and the musician Chopin conform to the real Sand's image of him as a "poor, sad angel," but very unhappy when he turns to polonaises because she feels "excluded" by the man who writes them: she cannot bear to play second fiddle to another woman—not even to Mother Poland. (Schumann described Chopin's music as "cannons buried under flowers!") Sand's two children (Maurice and Solange) are entirely written out of the film, incidentally.

In the event, the big dramatic moment in the film comes when Chopin learns that two of his boyhood friends have been imprisoned and that the price of their freedom is to be purchased dear. He hems, he haws, he pours a purse containing Polish soil into his hand, and this last act finally recalls him to his finer nature—the nature he has shown to Liszt rather than the one Sand has attempted to cultivate. In an hysterical sequence, Chopin now goes on tour to raise money for the cause even though he is dying of consumption (in fact, he may have had cystic fibrosis): he plays in Amsterdam and Berlin, Budapest and London, Paris and Stockholm, and, most hilariously of all, in Rome (a program of waltzes at the "Palace Theater"). This tour is a complete and utter fabrication, of course: Chopin never traveled to Holland, Hungary, or Italy (though he wrote the most marvelous of all barcaroles). On 16 November 1848, however, in London's Guildhall, he did play at the Polish Ball and Concert. Liszt, in his biography of the composer, called these performances "a final expression of love extended to his country, a final glance, a final sigh, a final sorrow!" American war-time audiences got the movie's message, and no doubt felt genuinely sad when the young composer gave up the ghost—as Liszt, in the background of the operatically staged deathbed scene, played his somber and majestic nocturne, opus 48, no. 1.

Cornel Wilde was, if not musical, at least a strong and clean-cut boy. If such a boy was fighting for America, the movie seemed to say, all would be right in the end; his death, if it should come (as Chopin's did in the film) in the line of duty, would be noble. In the event, *A Song to Remember* at least refuted the entrenched false conception of Chopin and his music as merely pretty or feminine (the ultimate in misogynistic invective), to which Said also made a contribution. In fact, Chopin's music, like Beethoven's and Mozart's and Schubert's, possessed a quality of sweetness even at the end, and because this is the quality most easily destroyed by life, reduced to flintiness and cynicism, it is perhaps the most precious.

12.

"The pianola 'replaces' Sappho's barbitos"

In the first years of the twentieth century, many pianists and composer-pianists fed the vogue for piano rolls by going into the recording studio. These rolls were made on a specially adapted piano that scored, or perforated, the paper roll with the general specifics of the original performance: the notes, obviously, but also a semblance of phrasing, tempo, pedaling, and dynamics. (Schnabel was among those who could not be induced to record this way. When told that the apparatus could capture something like sixteen dynamic grades, he responded that, unfortunately, he had seventeen.[1]) Later, a specially adapted piano (re-)played these rolls and so brought (non-amateur) music into middle-class houses—as, later, the phonograph would do with greater variety—as well as into concert halls. Bauer, who made a roll of a Saint-Saëns concerto, was present at its première at the Academy of Music in Philadelphia under Stokowski and the Philadelphia Orchestra:

> I still recall with a shudder the strange feeling I experienced when, the lid of the piano having been raised and the orchestra and Stokowski having taken their places, the manager came forward and said that Mr. Harold Bauer would now play the Saint-Saëns Concerto in G minor [no. 2]. 'You will see Mr. Bauer sitting in that box,' he continued, motioning toward me.

1. Neuhaus maintained that it is possible to produce one hundred dynamic grades on the piano, although there are indications for only about a tenth of them.

In the end, this "technology" was too unsophisticated, too approximate, to offer the spontaneous quality of an actual performance. (Had Gould lived then, he no doubt would have been all for it.) Indeed, the pianist often had to make adjustments in his playing to accommodate the requirements of the "recording" process itself—adjustments that were often at odds with the way he actually played in concert. Also, the recording process sometimes left certain inadequacies that had to be straightened out by a technician without the involvement of the pianist. One critic heard a Liszt rhapsody performed first by Cortot in person, then from a roll made by Cortot and played on a reproducing piano, and declared that he could scarcely tell the difference between them. Such testimonials are, in any case, rare. Rosenthal, for instance, when asked if he played in his youth as he did on a certain piano roll, responded, "No, and neither did anyone else." Though 78s may offer an altogether truer "record" than piano rolls, they were too crude to permit pianists to play at their ease. Indeed, in order to accommodate the time constraints of early discs, a pianist might have to speed up his playing of a certain work to make it fit. Busoni described the hell of recording to his wife in a 1919 letter:

> They wanted the Faust Waltz (which lasts a good ten minutes), *but it was only to take four minutes!* That meant quickly cutting, patching and improvising, so that there should still be some sense left in it; watching the pedal (because it sounds so bad); thinking of certain notes which had to be stronger or weaker to please this devilish machine; not letting oneself go for fear of inaccuracies. . . .

For Godowsky the process was even worse:

> The fear of doing a trifling wrong augmented while playing; the better one succeeded in playing the foregoing, the greater the fear became while playing. It was a dreadful ordeal, increasingly so the more sensitive the artist, I broke down in my health in London in the Spring of 1930, owing to these nerve-killing tortures. How can one think of emotion!

Indeed, Busoni and Godowsky were not alone in seeing something nefarious in the new gadgetry. Bauer again:

My good friend, Monsieur Blondel, head of the great French piano firm, Érard, was accustomed to say that the invasion of the machine into fields distinguished by fine handiwork was an unmixed evil, destructive to our civilization. He was totally opposed to modern devices applied to the manufacture of pianos. I frequently heard him deplore the introduction of the typewriter, which, he said, represented the beginning of the end ... because it substituted an impersonal mechanism for the refinement always needed in human intercourse. . . .

Sorabji, naturally, hoped the player piano would put an end to the virtuoso—or to the virtuoso's alleged vanity—since the player piano could be made to do things that no real (that is, living) musician could, or would, do. (Honegger was more or less of the same mind.) What Sorabji would not see was that it is not perfection *per se* that compels, but the spectacle of human achievement approaching, possibly touching, it. Stephen Jay Gould briefly addresses music in *Life's Grandeur: The Spread of Excellence from Plato to Darwin.* His apprehension of the virtuoso—unlike Sorabji's—is not redeemed by contradiction. For Sorabji, again, the virtuoso was not only as dangerous as the devil, but just as seductive. (To reiterate: his *Opus clavicembalisticum* was not written for, and is not playable by, any but the most diabolically gifted virtuoso.) For Gould, by contrast, the virtuoso need be neither courted nor pulled down from vainglorious heights, because, in fact, he does not inhabit them. No artist can agree with Gould's declaration that "he needn't improve on his past perfection, or exceed someone else's exceedingly rare achievement" because transcendence—of his materials, of himself—is written by the artist in his own life's blood. Failure to transcend is immaterial; to try is not.

* * *

Writers have been quick to react against the player piano as a symbol of the devolution of human feeling and expression, if not as a devolution of music itself. Benson condemns the pianola in *The Challoners,* and Pound writes of it in *Hugh Selwyn Mauberly: E. P. Ode pour l'élection de son sépulchre* (that masterful attempt to compress the James novel):

> The tea-rose tea-gown, etc.
> Supplants the mousseline of Cos,
> The pianola "replaces"
> Sappho's barbitos.[2]

Of course, the piano in general has a greater presence in poetry than the Pianola does. In Lawrence's "Piano" poem (the later version of the poem titled "The Piano"), even the memory of an inferior instrument makes the poet weep—

> In spite of myself, the insidious mastery of song
> Betrays me back, till the heart of me weeps to belong
> To the old Sunday evenings at home, with winter outside
> And hymns in the cosy parlour, the tinkling piano our guide.[3]

The most sustained criticism of the Pianola in literature comes in Forster's posthumously published novel *Maurice*. Here Clive Durham, the boy with whom Maurice falls in love up at Cambridge, is found in chapter six sorting out "a castle of pianola records" of the march from Tchaikovsky's *Pathétique;* then, when he goes to play them, a mutual friend tells Maurice, "you should get away from the machine [Pianola]"—and therefore Clive himself—"as far as you can." The Pianola manufactures music in the same way that Clive "manufactures" heterosexual passion (with consequences less outwardly disastrous for him than for Tchaikovsky). That the way one makes music—or connects to music—signifies one's values in Forster's work is illustrated beautifully when Maurice meets Alec Scudder at Penge: together they move a real piano from under a leak in Clive's ancestral home. This instrument, like their relationship, is the genuine article, and worth protecting from the decay of that society. The instrument itself embodies virtue.

In the event, the player piano as what was, in effect, a recording medium had gone the way of all earthly things by 1935. The real legacy of the instrument is the body of works composed directly for it: John Adams's *Grand Pianola Music* (1982), Hin-

---

2. The *barbitos* (or *barbiton*) is a many-stringed instrument; here, a lyre.

3. Robert Pinsky, too, remembers an imperfect instrument in "The Green Piano." After it has been replaced by "a crappy little Baldwin Acrosonic," the poet cries, "You were gone, despoiled one— / Pink one, forever green one, white-and-gold one, comforter, living soul."

demith's rondo and toccata, Nancarrow's *37 Studies for Player Piano* (1950-1968), Ernest Toch's *Études*, and Stravinsky's adaptations of his best-known pieces.

The Japanese firm of Yamaha makes "real" pianos—Richter played its model CFIIIS—as well as a reproducing model called the "Disklavier," and its advertisements and catalogues for the instruments underscore the distinction between the virtuoso and the virtuoso impostor as well as the distinction in *Maurice* between music played on a piano and by a Pianola. (It also realizes the fears of Érard's Monsieur Blondel.) An advertisement reads "The concert season at 930 Morningstar Lane will feature George Gershwin, Liberace, Chick Corea, and the Yamaha Disklavier piano." The omission of Kissin from the season roster suggests three possibilities: that his fee was too high; that he was booked when the Hendersons, the residents of 930 Morningstar Lane, put their concert series together; or that such a milieu—the advertisement features a photograph of the Hendersons' generic-looking house, and another of three generic-looking couples (one of them, presumably, the Hendersons) marveling over the Disklavier's performance—is hostile to musical truth. Obviously Possibility Three is the one that obtains. For the Hendersons, the Disklavier is an invention on the order of the vibrating bed or the talking car alarm: a notion. *La realtà dell'arte,* or "The Reality of the Art," as the catalogue of "real" pianos is titled, pictures a grand piano in a magnificent church, basking in a nimbus of celestial light. (A recent Kawai advertisement shows a grand piano lit from the same Source.) The Disklavier, by contrast, is photographed only in secular *tableaux:* a young couple dines while a vertical Disklavier plays itself; another Disklavier (this time a grand) "accompanies" a ballet lesson. The oddest *tableau* of all, however, is surely the first in the catalogue. In a paneled, softly lit, and utterly characterless room, a Disklavier plays for men who look like Rotarians and their consorts, who look like anchorwomen—all of them are drinking tea, eating biscuits, and chatting amiably. Although the party are not paying attention to the music, a young woman in a floral-patterned dress—a cultural super-ego for the assembled?—stands in front of a fireplace without a fire, holding a bouquet of plastic-wrapped roses in her

arms; flowers she seems to be waiting to present to the Disklavier
once it has finished playing its song. It is a powerful and complex
allegory.

In the seventh chapter of Frank Norris's *The Pit* (1903), there is a
disturbing displacement of the piano, though not by the pianola.
Laura (Mrs. Curtis Jadwin), in a funk over the disparity between
the actual nature of her married life and her cherished illusions
of romantic love, summons a former suitor, Sheldon Corthell, to
visit her. The artistic and urbane Corthell, aware of Laura's discontent, as well as—for all her romantic flights—her thralldom
to convention, works out a virtuoso musical plan whereby (he
hopes) she will allow herself to be seduced by him.

As Fate would have it, the Jadwin residence is furnished not
with a piano, but only with an organ. Thus, Corthell's sequence
of seductive piano works—Mendelssohn-Bartholdy's "Consolation" (opus 30, no. 3), the second movement of Beethoven's
"Appassionata," then Liszt's first *Mephisto* waltz—coupled (so to
speak) with heightened sexual tension, creates a kind of disori-
entation when played on an instrument so foreign to the repertoire. As the organ always has something of the church about it,
one suspects that, even had Laura's husband not returned home
at a decisive moment, she would have remained inviolate. Those
Victorian organ tones were too thick to permit of any trespass.

Had Corthell had a piano, who knows how far he might have
gotten?

13.

Musical Chairs; or,

Il virtuoso seduto

When we examine the correct way to sit at the
piano we have to deal with two sets of factors:
with the constant and with the variable. The
constants include the size and shape of the piano
and the height of the keyboard. The variables
include all the things that relate to the performer.
Not only his height and weight, but the infinite
diversity within the proportions of his anatomy
vary tremendously. The shape and size of his
fingers, hands, forearm, arm, torso—all these
influence the ideal sitting position.

—*György Sándor,* On Piano Playing

* * *

It may seem paradoxical that some pianists spend
more time choosing a chair for a concert than an
instrument: the piano technician at the Festival
Hall in London told me that the late Shura
Cherkassky decided on the piano he wanted in
five minutes, but spent twenty minutes trying out
different stools.

—*Charles Rosen, "On Playing the Piano"*

In the introduction to an anthology of Glenn Gould's writings,
Tim Page observes that the ecstasy-loving pianist "favored a very

low seating and inevitably brought along his own traveling folding chair to concerts, which set him at about eye level with the keyboard." (This chair was built for him by his father.)

Awadagin Pratt, who won the Naumburg Award in 1992, was inspired by Gould's example to experiment with low seating. He discovered that it allowed him to keep his wrists optimally relaxed, so he sits on a seemingly impossibly low hand-carved wooden stool when he plays.

Of Pachmann, Cardus wrote that "For all his eccentricities of personal behaviour on the piano stool (which I am told he reserved for English audiences), he was a purist of the instrument." Schonberg (*The Great Pianists*):

> One of his tricks was to raise [the stool], lower it, fiddle around with the controls until the audience was desperate. Then he would rush into the wings and come out with a large book, placing it on the seat. No good. Then he would rip out one page, put that page on the seat, and smile beatifically at the audience. Now he was comfortable.

Nabokov wrote a short story titled "Bachmann" in 1924; later he expressed surprise upon being told that "a pianist existed with some of my invented musician's peculiar traits" as well as a name that rhymed with Pachmann.

> Bachmann would walk onstage rapidly, as if escaping from an enemy or simply from irksome hands. Ignoring the audience, he would hurry up to the piano and, bending over the round stool, would begin tenderly turning the wooden disc of the seat, seeking a certain mathematically precise level. All the while he would coo, softly and earnestly, appealing to the stool in three languages. He would go on fussing thus for quite a while. English audiences were touched, French, diverted, German, annoyed. When he found the right level, Bachmann would give the stool a loving little pat and seat himself, feeling for the pedals with the soles of his ancient pumps. . . . At last he would bring his hands down softly onto the keys. Suddenly, though, a tortured little muscle would twitch under one eye; clucking his tongue, he would climb off the stool and again begin rotating its tenderly creaking disc.

From *The Journal of a Disappointed Man* by W. N. P. Barbellion (whose real name was Bruce Frederick Cummings), on a Pachmann concert at the Queen's Hall, London, in May 1916:

As usual he kept us waiting for 10 minutes. Then a short, fat, middle-aged man strolled casually on to the platform and everyone clapped violently—so it was Pachmann: a dirty greasy looking fellow with long hair of dirty grey colour, reaching down to his shoulders and an ugly face. He beamed on us and then shrugged his shoulders and went on shrugging them until his eye caught the music stool, which seemed to fill him with amazement. He stalked it carefully, held out one hand to it caressingly, and finding all was well, went two steps backwards, clasping his hands before him and always gazing at the little stool in mute admiration, his eyes sparkling with pleasure, like Mr Pickwick's on the discovery of the archæological treasure. He approached once more, bent down and ever so gently moved it about 7/8ths of an inch nearer the piano. He then gave it a final pat with his right hand and sat down.

Paderewski (*The Paderewski Memoirs*):

Now, in all my talks about the piano, I have neglected one of the most important things of all—*my* piano stool, which is a very special affair. It is both an invention and an innovation. It took me years to discover why I did not feel at ease when playing in public. There was always something wrong. A certain nervousness in my back which imposed a great strain upon me. I began to realize that my piano stool was the difficulty. I was always searching for the right piano stool. I experimented with one after another and tried, I suppose, hundreds of stools in what was beginning to seem an unending search. Finally, quite unexpectedly, I found one at Érard's in Paris which was agreeable to me. It was the lowest one they had; in fact the lowest one I had ever seen up to that moment, and it proved to be the perfect piano stool for me.

(Paderewski's piano stool makes an appearance in the opening concert sequence of *Moonlight Sonata*.)

Harold Taylor (*Kentner: A Symposium*):

He has one idiosyncrasy: the little blue piano stool with detachable legs which always travels with him; ordinary music stools do not wind low enough for his comfort. Yet should this be regarded as an idiosyncrasy? Piano playing is a sedentary occupation, and no one demonstrates the relationship between fine sitting and fine playing more precisely than Louis Kentner.

From *Piano Competition: The Story of the Leeds:* "One girl would only play if she could have a red piano stool."

From Piero Rattalino's note to the volume of the Philip's Great Pianists of the Twentieth Century series devoted to Radu Lupu:

> The fact that Lupu used an ordinary chair with a backrest, instead of a piano stool, made his attitude to the piano seem at the very least unusual. He needed such a chair because he leaned on it frequently. From a visual point of view Lupu contradicted a principle of fine tone: if the back is relaxed, a major part of the arm's weight dissipates on the seat of the body instead of on the keyboard. The position chosen by Lupu was due neither to eccentricity nor to a weakness of the dorsal muscles, but was designed instead to help in his search for tone colour.

Former child prodigy Ruth Slenczynska (author of *Forbidden Childhood*, a harrowing autobiography) in *Music at Your Fingertips:*

> I put telephone books on my chair to give myself a different position; then, again, I play the same piece sitting on a low kitchen stool. I have to do something similar all the time on tour. Every pianist has a favourite height for his keyboard, and practically all pianoforte stools are adjustable, but sometimes the exertion of playing a particular pianoforte requires a different body position. Also, the change of seating height helps me to "loosen up," to get a free, unhampered feeling.

Horowitz, in the thirties, ordered piano benches from the firm of Schmieg and Kotzian because those made for him by Steinway—upholstered benches, forty-eight inches long and seventeen inches high—were, as Schonberg recalls the pianist's wife as saying, "ruining his concerts."

> The minutest details were discussed, down to adjustable mechanism that would work in increments of a thousandth of an inch. The price came to $500 per bench. At that time many people in America were not earning that much in a year. Horowitz gulped, but ordered two.

From *The Biography of Leopold de Meyer:*

> As usual he had sent his grand piano before him with the legs unscrewed, and the Turks [this was in Constantinople], not understanding the utility of these partitions of furniture, they be-

ing accustomed on all occasions to sit on ottomans, could not conceive how the instrument should be raised to permit the performer to play. At last five Turks were summoned, who were ordered to place themselves on all fours, and the piano being laid horizontally on their backs, they thought would afford a sufficient elevation to the player. Léopold de Meyer's entrance set all to rights, and released the poor Turks from their 'durance vile.'

From *The Sins of the Cities of the Plain, or The Recollections of a Mary-Ann*, the memoirs of Jack Saul, a "professional sodomite" in Victorian London:

> He rose from the breakfast-table, and opening the piano, ran his fingers over the keys; then motioning me to come to him, gave me a luscious kiss. 'You darling Eveline. . . . Now I will play you a nice piece, only I have a fancy to have you in me. . . .' he said, as he made me sit on the music-stool, then raised my dress, and turning his bottom to me, lifted his own clothes and gradually sat down in my lap . . . and he began to play and sing 'Don't you remember sweet Alice, Ben Bolt?' from a parody in the *Pearl Magazine*,[1] which he had set to music.

* * *

Kentner (from *Piano*): "Clearly no conclusions can be drawn about a pianist's technique from the height of his seat."

1. *The Pearl, A Journal of Facetive and Voluptuous Reading* was published monthly from July 1879 to December 1880. The parody in question appeared in September 1880 (issue no. 15) under the title "Sweet Polly." It begins like this:

> Oh, do you remember Sweet Polly, Ben Bolt,
> Sweet Polly with a cunt soft and brown;
> How she'd grin with delight when you gave her a quid,
> And how quickly she'd fetch a prick down?

As for "Ben Bolt" proper (words by Thomas Dunn English, music by R. Sinclair): it was a popular song on both sides of the Atlantic for at least three decades.

14.

"Aut Caesar, aut nihil"

Van Cliburn's triumph at the first Tchaikovsky Competition in Moscow, on 13 April 1958, was politically of enormous consequence. His was the symbolic victory of Americanism over Communism—Khrushchev hugged him, both Gilels (who had played in America for the first time only in 1955) and Richter (who would not play in America until 1960) praised him—and he became the first musician in the history of the United States to be honored with a ticker-tape parade down Broadway. (The only American to have made such political moment abroad before Cliburn was Jesse Owens, at the 1936 Olympic Games in Berlin.) Further, what Kaiser described as his "beautifully and lyrically sincere, but probably hardly unique or incomparable" recording of Tchaikovsky's first concerto—Cold War-horse of Cold War-horses—was the first classical recording to sell more than one million copies.

Chasins's *The Van Cliburn Legend*, which records these events, is among other things a fascinating work of propaganda. Clearly, Chasins's personal mission was to establish the articulate and photogenic Cliburn first as a fine American boy, and second as a fine musician. I do not know Cliburn personally, and have no more reason to doubt those of his virtues that Chasins commends—studiousness, temperance, patriotism, devotion to his mother, Christianity—than I have to believe in them. Regardless of such personal qualities, however, he was not, in the end, a great pianist for the simple reason that he did not continue to develop as a musician in his middle and early old age. At first he played his chosen repertoire very well (and with magnificent tone); then he began to play the same repertoire less well. In time, even his studio recordings became pocked with misreadings. Cliburn never accompanied singers or played chamber music (in contrast to Argerich, Arrau, Ashkenazy, Barenboim, Cortot, Curzon, Fischer, Gilels, Hess, Horowitz, Kempff, Kissin, Lipatti, Richter, Rubinstein, and Serkin, for example), and finally stopped recording (and for the most part playing in public) altogether. In this regard, he was the opposite of Gould, who gave his last concert—comprising four fugues from Bach's *Art of Fugue* and the same composer's fourth partita, Beethoven's sonata opus 110, and Hindemith's third sonata—in Los Angeles, on 10 April 1964, and thereafter *only* recorded.[1] On several occasions during the 1990s Cliburn performed concerti (Liszt, Rachmaninov, Tchaikovsky), but these concerts in no way burnished his reputation.[2]

Early in Cliburn's career, which was impressive even before his victory in Moscow, Szell (who was himself an excellent pianist) noted that the Texan was "no philosopher." For that matter, Chasins himself conceded that Cliburn was no better than many other American *virtuosi:*

> Comparisons are usually misleading, because artistry is as unduplicable as people. But here, I think, an exchange typical of many I've had might serve some useful purpose.
>
> 'Is Cliburn a better musician than Seymour Lipkin or Jacob Lateiner?'[3]
> 'No.'
> 'Is he a better technician than Byron Janis or John Browning?'[4]
> 'No.'

1. Gould's decision to retire from the concert stage after nine years echoes Liszt's decision to leave it at the end of his eight "Years of Transcendental Execution." Notwithstanding his antagonistic interpretations of the Romantic repertoire, Gould was an essentially Romantic pianist.
2. In 1998, he was among the first musicians to play in the new Bass Performance Hall in Fort Worth: he gave his first local recital in decades, playing music of Brahms, Debussy, and Chopin that he had also, alas, recorded decades earlier. Several days before, however, in the inaugural concert in the hall, he had broken new ground by accompanying mezzo-soprano Frederica von Stade.
3. Both Lipkin and Lateiner studied at the Curtis Institute of Music in Philadelphia; the former with Serkin, the latter with Isabelle Vengerova. Lipkin won the Rachmaninov competition the only time it was held.
4. Janis is the most eminent of Horowitz's acknowledged pupils. In the 1970s, psoriatic arthritis forced him into retirement, yet two decades later he was

'Has he more repertoire or a wider range of color and style than Gary Graffman or Leon Fleisher?'[5]
'No.'
'Has he more intellectual understanding than Eugene Istomin or Claude Frank?'[6]
'No.'
'Well, then, what gives?'
It's an excellent question. . . .

—Chasins's answer to which is Cliburn's vaunted "emotional style"; a style that Cliburn could not sustain—and that some European critics did not grant in the first place.

After the Tchaikovsky Competition, Cliburn became best known for the quadrennial piano competition in Fort Worth, Texas, that bears his name and that was inaugurated in 1962 to honor his victory in Moscow: a competition, it must be noted, that brings diminishing returns both to itself and to its participants with each running. Nonetheless the Cliburn remains, if not in relevance then at least in profile, the epitome of the modern piano competition.[7]

The modern competition—the purpose of which is to award a first prize to an alleged virtuoso who will go on to have a high-profile career—pays a poor tribute to what Hildebrandt calls "the rich tradition of duels" at the keyboard: J. S. Bach *v.* Jean Louis Marchand (1717), Händel *v.* Scarlatti (brought together in Rome, in Cardinal Ottoboni's salon), Clementi *v.* Mozart (Vienna, 1781), Beethoven *v.* Daniel Steibelt (1800), and Liszt *v.* Sigismond Thal-

able to resume recording and concertising once again. (He gave a recital at Alice Tully Hall on 29 October 1998 to mark the fiftieth anniversary of his Carnegie Hall [recital] debut.) Browning won the Leventritt competition in 1955 (Cliburn had won it the year before), and in 1962 he gave the world premiere of the Barber piano concerto.

5. Both Graffman and Fleisher were deprived of the use of their right hand and subsequently turned to the repertoire for the left hand alone. Graffman, who studied at Curtis with Vengerova, won the Leventritt in 1949. Both pianists made significant recordings with Szell and the Cleveland Orchestra when they played bimanually.

6. Istomin, who studied at Curtis with Serkin and won the Leventritt in 1943, is best known for his performances with the trio he formed with cellist Leonard Rose and violinist Isaac Stern. Frank was yet another Schnabel pupil.

7. Joseph Horowitz's *The Ivory Trade* is a thorough and important history of the competition.

berg (Paris, 1837). Bach,[8] Mozart, Beethoven, and Liszt won their respective contests, and Händel *v.* Scarlatti was a tie because the German won in organ playing while the Italian won in harpsichord playing. Nonetheless these "trials of skill" produced judgments that remain valid and instructive. A contemporary account of Bach *v.* Marchand concluded, "Pompey was not necessarily a bad general merely because he lost the battle of Pharsalus to Caesar," while Liszt *v.* Thalberg was *almost* a contest between Rome and Carthage. In every case, the protagonists were more evenly matched than the entrants in any modern competition could ever hope to be. We would have to put Argerich against Zimerman, or Pletnev (who, in a 1997 interview, pronounced himself "the best living pianist") against Pogorelich (who has said that he, Horowitz, and Rachmaninov were the century's most important pianists; ergo, he is the best living pianist), to witness such glamorous and fair "trials of skill" again.

What the Cliburn jury (but not *only* the Cliburn jury) requires is a victor who springs, like Athena, fully armed from the head of Jove—a master of all styles, equally at home playing recitals, chamber music and concerti (an "inhuman rather than superhuman" demand, as Kaiser bravely and fairly writes), who is not necessarily objectively superior, but only better than the also-rans. (The Cliburn has never not awarded its first prize. The Leventritt juries, by contrast, refused to name a winner when no pianist met its standards for that honor. No winner was named in 1942, 1950, 1960, 1971, or 1976, the year the competition was discontinued. The Chopin and Tchaikovsky competitions have also withheld their first prizes.) The maximum age for competitors in piano competitions is usually somewhere between thirty and thirty-five, yet how many pianists can have had time by that age to become finished artists? I often wonder why no competition sets a *minimum* age limit of thirty or thirty-five for competitors. It might be said that competitions, like youth, are wasted on the young.

At present there are hundreds of piano competitions; con-

---

8. According to some sources, there was no "duel" between Bach and Marchand (the organist at Versailles); the Frenchman, certain of humiliation, having decamped from Dresden on the morning of the contest.

tests named for composers (Beethoven, Busoni, Hummel, Liszt, Schubert, . . .) and patrons (Reine Elisabeth de Belgique, Walter W. Naumburg, . . .), cities (Cleveland, Dublin, Hamamatsu, Munich, Palm Beach, . . .) and pianists (Anda, Casadesus, Haskil, William Kapell, José Vianna da Motta, . . .). Almost every notable pianist born after the Second World War has won a prize—or has notably *not* won a prize—in at least one of these contests. Even so, few of those whose subsequent careers have proven them to be truly outstanding pianists are often remembered as competition winners: though Argerich won the Chopin, and Michelangeli and Solti the Geneva, it is not as such that we think of them. In my mind, and possibly for other people, "competition winner" is more likely to evoke a conservatory-trained pianist in his or her twenties with an uncertain artistic and probably dismal professional (that is, public) future, than a virtuoso of the first order.

I have lately heard prize winners from a number of competitions. Two of them—Simone Pedroni (1993 Cliburn) and Eldar Nebolsin (1992 Santander)—exemplify the arbitrariness, the hasty certification, almost endemic to international competitions, and to the more famous contests in particular.

The first of Pedroni's programs that I heard began with Bach's G major *adagio*, BWV 968, then moved, without pause, into the same composer's third *English* suite. After their preludes, the *English* suites are comprised of dance movements, but Pedroni managed to omit any expression of the dance, of beautiful and formal (even stylized) motion. (The sarabande was the only thing Pedroni played that revealed any sense of imagination: I kept expecting the *recitativo* from the third movement of Schumann's F-sharp minor sonata to erupt from it, and for me this "worked.") Demonstrating a weakness for suites, he rounded out the first half of his concert with Schoenberg's opus 25. Gould placed this "among the most spontaneous and wickedly inventive of Schoenberg's works," so I was pleased that Pedroni was able to dispatch it, at least, with some flair.

After the intermission, Pedroni essayed Rachmaninov's *Cinq morceaux de Fantasie*, opus 3 and second sonata (1931 version). The second of these pieces is the prelude that became an albatross around the composer's neck because "it," as he himself called the prelude, was always demanded of him as an encore: without exaggeration, it is the most famous thing Rachmaninov wrote; more, even, than the tune from the third movement of his second concerto later vulgarized as the song "Full Moon and Empty Arms." The familiarity of the work, rather than Pedroni's performance of it, brought the audience into better humor than it had been at the end of the first half. Then, in the sonata, a disaster that need not have been a disaster occurred: Pedroni had a severe memory lapse, but rather than start again or play from the score (to neither of which any shame need attend), he did the pianistic equivalent of doodling until he got back on track. The trouble was not that Pedroni lost his place, but that his attempt to "cover" his mistake was both coarse and disrespectful of his audience.[9] (He begged a degree of patience that few people in the theater were inclined to grant him, for he had shown neither greatness nor *simpatia*.)

This episode reminded me of two capital anecdotes. The first, about Liszt, was told by his Mississippi-born pupil Amy Fay. While "rolling up the piano in arpeggios in a very grand manner indeed," she recalled, Liszt

> struck a semi-tone short of the high note upon which he had intended to end. I caught my breath and wondered whether he was going to leave us like that, in mid-air, as it were, and the harmony unresolved, or whether he would be reduced to the humiliation of correcting himself like ordinary mortals, and taking the right chord. A half smile came over his face . . . and he instantly went meandering down the piano in harmony with the false note he had struck, and then rolled deliberately up in a second grand sweep, *this* time striking true. . . . Instead of giving you a chance to say, 'He has made a mistake,' he forced you to say, 'He has shown how to get out of a mistake.'

The second, concerning Pachmann, was told by Rosina Lhévinne.

9. Bernard Shaw "contracted an early prejudice" against von Bülow because when the pianist's memory failed "he used to improvise Schubertian basses in pieces by Handel with an unscrupulousness that ran through all his performances."

In the middle of a sonata, he compleley forgot where he was in the music. Without any hesitation, instead of going behind the stage, he went forward and up the aisle. He walked like a lunatic, [and] staring straight ahead he slowly went to the very back of the hall. There he jumped on a chair, reached up and stopped a clock and said in a loud voice that the ticking of the clock had disturbed him. Then he returned to the piano and resumed playing.

By the end of Pedroni's recital, the theater was half-empty. On this occasion, it was the music students in the upper seats, not the *borghesi* in the orchestra, who had decamped in frustration and irritation: the concert was unbearable if one knew the music. I myself stayed to the end only from a sense of duty.

Nebolsin seemed an altogether more serious pianist: his concert also began with Bach (*Italian Concerto*) and he played with more beauty of tone than did Pedroni; his *mezza voce* in the first movement was particularly lovely. Though his accounts of the other two movements of the Bach, and indeed all the works he chose (the *Chaconne* from 1962 by Sofia Gubaidulina, two Rachmaninov preludes from opus 23, and Prokofiev's sixth sonata) were sometimes accomplished, however, there were significant underlying problems; the most notable (in common with Pedroni) being an architectural formlessness. What organization he made of his sounds seemed unconscious, without being spontaneous or intuitive.

I had a strange impression the whole time I watched Nebolsin play: his hands did not seem to correspond in any way to the sounds they were producing from the beautiful Hamburg Steinway at which he was seated. Indeed, if I had not seen the moving hammers reflected in the lid of the instrument, I could have well believed that he was doing the pianistic equivalent of lip-synching. He seemed, that day, a very sad young man; all that was not fulfilling about his playing had an air of resigned intelligence. (Likewise, Nebolsin's recordings—the first of sonatas by Chopin and Liszt, the second of three Chopin works for piano and orchestra, conducted by Ashkenazy—fail to spark.)

Reflecting on the playing of these pianists (and several other prize-winners as well), I thought of a line from Ford Madox

Ford's novel *The Good Soldier:* "It is a queer and fantastic world. . . . The things were all there to content everybody; yet everybody has the wrong thing." The faculty by which the Romantic *virtuosi* attempted to make the music of all epochs intelligible to their era is all but lost.

The international piano competition, in the form that it has held sway, is changing, however—a sign that perhaps institutional authority in music is weakening; that only institutions themselves esteem what they dispense. The Tin Man in *The Wizard of Oz* may have become learned merely by possessing a diploma, but in our world a pianist is not usually made better just by winning a gold (or gold-toned) medal. Perahia's career took off only after he had a competition victory behind him; Cliburn's only after he had won the Tchaikovsky. Before going to Moscow, he had won five competitions—among them the Leventritt. This proves how arbitrary the recognition of talent can be. Thus while some contests have launched more important international careers than others—Argerich, Pollini, and Zimerman won the Chopin (Argerich also won the Busoni and Geneva competitions); Alexeev, Lupu, and Perahia the Leeds;[10] Ashkenazy, Fleisher, and Gilels the Queen Elisabeth (Brussels)—victory no longer assures international success. This is partially because competitions are themselves more (or too) numerous, and partially because the careers of competition victors have shown that winning in and of itself is of no inherent worth. It is perhaps only by regarding a competition victory from a Taoist perspective that any real satisfaction can be had. Yet who would submit to the psychological and physical tortures of a competition for a success that offers nothing save its own contemplation?

Throughout the history of the piano competition one fact has not changed: the competition is only as good as its jurors. In the most important competitions, jurors are mavericks—and as

10. The moving force behind the Leeds competition, Fanny Waterman, has both a strict anti-virtuoso bias and an unencouragingly mercantile view of art: "And it would be a bad thing if every competition kept on churning out Lupus and Perahias—there's simply not enough work to go round."

likely, if not more likely, to quarrel with fellow jurors than with competitors. Cortot, for example, dissociated himself from the jury of the Vienna competition in 1934 when Lipatti was not awarded first prize (Boleslav Kohn, who had won third prize at the 1932 Chopin competition, won it instead),[11] and Michelangeli resigned from the jury of the 1955 Chopin competition when Adam Harasiewicz, not Ashkenazy, won first prize. If competitors themselves are seldom mavericks, it is because winning a competition is a matter of winning over a jury: consensus obviates greatness, at least when the consensus is among jurors whose own careers have, as Gould diplomatically expressed it ("We Who Are About To Be Disqualified Salute You!"),

> attracted heretofore something less than universal renown. And it is, I am afraid, equally characteristic of musicians thwarted in their aspirations for international acclaim to decry the unaccountable mysteries of personality, to downgrade those virtues of temperamental independence which signal the genuine re-creative fire.

Like Gould, I have no patience with those *systems* which would confer authority, because true authority cannot be conferred, only taken. (The appeal of the Prometheus myth to musicians is hardly surprising.)

Egorov—who took prizes at the 1974 Tchaikovsky and 1975 Queen Elisabeth competitions—is the most famous non-winner of the Cliburn, yet that contest effectively launched his career. Impresario Maxim Gershunoff raised $10,000 from disappointed members of the 1977 audience so that Egorov—who had defected to the West the year before—could give the New York recital reserved for the competition's first prize winner. After Egorov played at Carnegie Hall for the first time, on 16 December 1978, Andrew Porter, writing in *The New Yorker,* called him "the biggest and most poetical young pianistic talent I have ever encountered." That year the second prize went to Alexander

11. Although Cortot considered Lipatti the greater pianist, his primary objection was to the *basis* upon which Kohn was given first prize: Kohn was close to the competition's age-limit, whereas Lipatti, at sixteen, just met the minimum age for competitors.

Toradze, and the first to Steven De Groote, a South African about whom John Ardoin, music critic of the *Dallas Morning News,* wrote for *The New York Times* on 9 October:

> A detractor . . . would describe [him] as an example of the classic contest winner—a superb and fluent mechanism coupled with a common-denominator approach to music which is solid but not revelatory, and which gives offense to no one except those expecting an immense personality, one to match the prize. . . .

English pianist Freddy Kempf (a relation of Wilhelm's) was head and shoulders above the other competitors at the 1998 Tchaikovsky competition—he was the audience's favorite as well —yet he was awarded only third prize. Tikhon Khrenikov, the jury chairman, threatened (twice) to resign, but in the end he stayed on and secured a special jury award for Kempf. The Tchaikovsky was conceived to demonstrate the superiority of Soviet pianists; notwithstanding the influence of the Soviet piano mafia, however, it has seldom been able to do so: Cliburn won in 1958 (with the eleventh-hour authorization of the Kremlin, forced by the audience's wild adoration of the young American), Ogdon and Ashkenazy jointly in 1962, John Lill and Vladimir Krainev jointly in 1970, Peter Donohoe and Vladimir Ovchinikov jointly the second prize—the first was not awarded—in 1982, and Barry Douglas in 1986.

Pogorelich is yet another virtuoso whose career was launched as a result of his not being advanced as far as the final round of the 1980 Chopin (though he had just won first prize in Montréal): half the jury gave him the highest number of possible points and the other gave him the lowest number. Argerich, one of those who gave him the highest number, resigned in protest, and Deutsche Grammaphon stepped in to sign him to an exclusive contract. Scandal, as is so often the case, proved itself to be the most felicitous kind of publicity. The notes to Pogorelich's first disc—a Chopin recital—read in part: "In bringing out contrasts to the full he does violence only to the sensibilities of conservative listeners, not to Chopin's text."

Dang Thai Son of Vietnam won first prize that year. Tatiana

Shebanova and Arutiun Papazian, both of the USSR, won second and third prize respectively.

The most fortunate pianist, in the way his career began, was Horowitz, who won no competitions: "I played some of my first concerts to almost empty halls at first, but then with each concert the hall became fuller and fuller. It's much better that way." (Horowitz also stipulated in his last will and testament that no piano competition should ever be named for him.) Kissin has won no competition either.

If someone writes a book about the winners of musical competitions, I have a title to offer: *The Gods that Failed*. A first prize is seen as the anointing of a holy of art, but gods are born, not made. It is idols that are made, and they always have feet of clay.

ARISTOCRACY

David and I went to an outdoor concert of the Orchestra of the Academy of Santa Cecilia a few days after we moved to Rome, and though it was perfectly pleasant to hear Mendelssohn-Bartholdy's incidental music to *A Midsummer Night's Dream* (and, afterwards, Respighi's *Fountains of Rome*) on a midsummer night at the Villa Giulia, the concert depended more on atmosphere than on musicianship: music was part of an experience that took in scenery and lighting (a lilac-colored dusk), and the noise of planes leaving from Fiumicino, and a chance encounter with friends in a grotto during intermission. This was an example of that particular affirmation of the familiar which Barthes called *plaisir.* Zimerman's playing of Chopin's B-flat minor sonata in Florence a few months earlier, by contrast, defined what Barthes called *jouissance;* the revelation of a famous composition as one of unknown terror, cogency and grandeur. In short, the former was a social occasion, an evocation of the eighteenth-century's *concerts champêtre;* the latter an aesthetic experience that bent time itself to its will.

Art is often held to be of value to the degree that it can be put to some sort of practical or social use, or to promote "social change." (Even more often, artworks are pronounced worthless because of their perceived undermining of social values.) Alternately, art is looked upon as a commodity that people purchase in order to beautify their homes, their communities, their social status within those communities, or their souls. Yet this latter argument—which seems to be in opposition to the former—is in fact its equally bourgeois corollary, since both press art into extra-artistic service.

The miracle of an aristocratic performance lies in its capacity to vaporize everything that surrounds it, and in particular all efforts to appropriate it. Thus, even though we were sitting in a theater when we heard Zimerman, surrounded by other people, program notes, red velvet, our own thoughts, perfume, for the duration of the sonata everything except the sonata ceased to be: each of us was alone with Zimerman, just as he was alone with Chopin.

15.

Muscles and Soul

I acknowledge only one morality, and that is the
morality of power.

—*Beethoven*

It is almost a commonplace that, if one were to draw up a list of
the foremost one hundred female pianists of the twentieth century and another of their foremost one hundred male counter-
parts, the latter would have a dramatically higher "recognition
factor" than the former. Whether this reflects an inherent sex-
ism in the music industry, or some genuine disparity between
the sexes so far as piano playing and interpretive ability is concerned, will remain a topic of debate. What is certain is that
women piano virtuosi constitute a minority.

At about the turn of the last century, Henry C. Lahee, in his
Famous Pianists of To-day and Yesterday, relegated women in a
chapter of their own—the last one. Robert Cowan, in the special
piano issue of *BBC Music Magazine*, placed only one woman
(Haskil) among "twenty of the very best," while in the same issue
Michael Church placed two women (Argerich and Uchida) in
his personal Top Ten of the greatest living pianists. Still in the
same issue, Jeremy Siepmann included only five discs by women
on his list of "Fifty recordings of superlative pianists past and
present." An *hors-série* edition (Autumn 1998) of *Le Monde de la
Musique* named about twenty-five recordings by women on its
list of the 180 CDs that make up "Le meilleur du piano," yet this
figure is misleading: de Larrocha is the author of six of these

twenty-five (predictably, all six are of Spanish music), Argerich of five, Marie-Catherine Girod of three, and Viktoria Postnikova of two. (That Anna Stella Schic's Villa-Lobos and Mariane Schroeder's Giacinto Scelsi merit their place among the "best of the piano" is extravagantly doubtful.) Finally, of the seventy-four pianists represented in *Great Pianists of the Twentieth Century* (Philips)—with 200 CDs the largest project in recording history—ten are women: Argerich, Haskil, Hess, de Larrocha, Uchida, Maria Yudina and—somewhat questionably—Ingrid Haebler, Rosina Lhévinne (primarily as an adjunct to her husband), Pires and Tureck. (That there is no Bachauer or Darré, no Landowska—playing Mozart and Haydn concertos on a piano—or Novaës, is scandalous.)[1] Again, is this chauvinism (and jingoism), or a genuine assessment of the talent pool?

A handful of writers have explained away women pianists, and women *virtuosi*, on the grounds of a lack of physical power. Sorabji, for instance, wrote in "Against Women Instrumentalists":

> narrow-chested, shallow bodies, bad carriage, emaciated arms, underdeveloped muscles, feeble tissues; they look like the poor, mean, thin, parched, anaemic sounds they produce from their instruments—pale, wan changelings of tone. They can in the very nature of things do no better, but it is preposterous even for such people to expect to become great players, or even good second-raters. . . . The physical weakness communicates itself to the playing, inevitably and inexorably, with the result that we get the feeble, debile, thoroughly depressing and sickly playing that ninety-nine out of a hundred women give us.

(While for Sorabji Frieda Kwast-Hoddap was the one out of a hundred, in his reviews for *The New English Weekly* he actually had good words for a number of female pianists. Of Eileen Joyce,

---

1. While I can understand the project director's reasons for giving a few pianists two or three issues in the edition (even as I disagree violently with some of the particular pianists paid this tribute—how can Brendel have three and Sofronitsky only one?), I must lament that seventy-four were included instead of one hundred. How much more significant the series would have been with the inclusion of a further twenty-six pianists—not only Bachauer and Darré, Landowska and Novaës, but Nyiregyházi and Raymond Lewenthal (a finer player of Alkan and Liszt than Odgon, who gets two issues), Lazar Berman and Youri Egorov.

whom he heard play Busoni's *Indian Fantasy* in 1934, he wrote, "praise be to all the Gods and Devils, [her] playing is utterly free from 'feminine charm' . . . it is so excellent that no damning excuse of that sort has to be made for it." Darré and Hephzibah Menuhin received the balm of his praise as well.)

Though Sorabji's disdain for women pianists is almost comically over-the-top, more measured critics make the same point: power—specifically, controlled power—is a requirement for which no other quality can be substituted. When Rosenthal played Liszt's *Réminiscences de Don Juan* in Manchester, on 23 November 1900, Johnstone wrote:

> He hurled forth the Dionysiac declaration of war against all the chilly conventions and proprieties, the priggeries and pruderies of Mrs. Grundy, that forms the real content of the piece, with that technical power in which he is surpassed by no living performer.

Illustrating that virtuosity is as much a matter of refinement and nuance, Rosenthal followed this performance with one of Chopin's *Berceuse*, "bringing out all the delicate moonshine filigree of the right-hand part with infinite subtlety." This, too, he learned from Liszt, whose "embellishments were like a cobweb—so fine —or like the texture of costliest lace."

Hanslick, on the other hand, reviewing a concert by Clara Schumann in Vienna (1856), wrote:

> The effect of her playing is never to overpower or to transport. It is a most truthful representation of magnificent compositions, but not an outpouring of a magnificent personality. This is not only more appropriate to the true task of virtuosity; it is also its fulfillment, and we should be compelled to declare her playing ideal, if everything human were not imperfect, and if every virtue did not have its deficiencies.
>
> She could be called the greatest living pianist rather than merely the greatest female pianist, were the range of her physical strength not limited by her sex. The compelling power of a pianist resides principally in his touch. Only he who can draw the full tone from the instrument can project the full impression, be it in the tempest of an allegro or in the long-drawn cantilena of an adagio. Every personal artistic performance, as a twin product of body and mind, must obey the terms of both, and one need not be a musical Karl Vogt to find the effective

power of a pianist more in the muscles of his hand than in the greatness of his soul.

Is the important role that so many (mostly male) critics grant to physical power in piano playing the articulation of a harsh physiological reality, or merely a tactic by which to trivialize women pianists? The answer to this crucial question is not entirely clear, although it is curious to note that nothing resembling a feminist ethos exists in the piano world; even today, most women pianists consider being told "you play like a man" a compliment. (Equally, male critics consider telling a woman that she plays like a man a compliment.)[2] Obviously some women have a feeling against their sex in the same way that some homosexuals are homophobic; yet the history of piano playing suggests that such negative feeling is present in women pianists almost to a one. Why is this? Is the fact that so many women *virtuosi* elect to compete with men in repertoire in which they are usually at a disadvantage due simply to a desire to prove themselves the equals of men: to prove that their sex is *not* a handicap? If so, such a premise is as self-defeating as it is at odds with that school of feminism that urges women to create their own canons, and that in literature was largely responsible for the rediscovery of Virginia Woolf in the 1960s.

In my entire concertgoing life I have never heard a woman pianist play in concert even a single composition written by another woman, though I have heard several men do so—and I know that Virginia Eskin, for one, does so. Likewise, with the exception of Argerich (who favors a skirt and leotard top, both in black, and often some kind of loose jacket as well) and Uchida (whose brother is a fashion designer), I have rarely seen a woman pianist costume herself in anything other than a dress or skirt when playing a concert; another curious abnegation of feminist dogma—and practicality.

Couture has been an interesting aspect of recitals by women,

2. In his note to Juana Zayas's CD of the Chopin *études*, C. J. Lutens writes:

Why is Juana Zayas so little known? In short, for the same reason the great Italian pianist Maria Tipo was virtually unknown less than a decade ago. Each of these artists nobly chose to forgo their well-launched careers in order to respond to the loftier calling of motherhood.

or concerts in which women appear, for decades. Deems Taylor, for one, could not but help but "wonder whether some of them are more interested in music or dressmaking . . . here are ladies trailing clouds of flame-colored chiffon or dazzling in silks and spangles." (For his part, Shaw remembered that Arabella Goddard "wore wide hanging sleeves long after everybody else had given them up, and that they gave a certain winged grace to the travelling to and fro of her elbows. . . .") And while a concert of works by Clara Schumann and a pants outfit do not a female-positive musician make, it does seem odd that by this point a revolution of some kind has not taken place among women in the piano world.

Because I am a man, I cannot presume to set forth the parameters of this revolution. I can, however, wish hopefully for the opportunity to hear the sonatas of Maria Theresia von Paradis, who, though blind from her fifth year, became a respected composer, singer and pianist for whom no less august a figure than Mozart wrote a concerto. I can wish for a revival of interest in Delphine Hill Handley (née Schauroth), a pianist and composer to whom Mendelssohn dedicated his G minor concerto and of whom Schumann prophesied, "she will develop into a romanticist, and then, with Clara, we would have two amazons in the glittering array." I can wish for performances of Clara's cadenzas to Beethoven's third and fourth concerti and Mozart's D minor concerto, K. 466, or for concerts of her own works, since they are practically unknown (save by echo in Robert's music), and since Schumann's "encouragement" of her work even before their marriage in 1840 was conditioned by a sexist mentality. "Florestan and Eusebius," in a collective review titled "The Museum" (12 September 1837), concluded that her *Soirées musicales*, opus 6 contained qualities that "one is accustomed to expect only from experienced artists—and males!" (Schumann also had no reservations about the professional sacrifices that Clara was compelled to make in order to give birth to their eight children.)

McClary explains the minimal presence of women pianists in the contemporary music world as follows:

> Most males have experienced the anxiety that if they're musicians, that must mean they're sissies. So on the professional level, music—like cuisine or clothing design—necessarily becomes *men's* work. This has been especially true with the piano

because of its strong traditional association with women. Which means that if you want piano playing to be a respectable male profession, you have to agree that it's something women can't really do.

This is, finally, a facile and preëmptive argument. It is, of course, undeniable that piano playing has a "strong traditional association" with women, *but only at the amateur level*. Loesser, for one, pays due tribute to those few women who contributed to the art of the piano as either performers or muses, while noting that non-keyboard instruments have historically been regarded as unsuitable to both a woman's dignity and physiognomy.

> When a woman plays the flute, she must purse her lips; and she must do so likewise when she blows a horn, besides also giving evidences of visceral support for her tone. What encouragement might that not give the lewd-minded among her beholders? When she plays a cello, she must spread her legs: perish the thought! "In thousands of people it calls up pictures that it ought not to call up," primly said the anonymous *Musikalischer Almanach für 1784*. When she plays the violin, she must twist her upper torso and strain her neck in an unnatural way; and if she practices much, she may develop an unsightly scar under her jaw.

Further, he laments the inappropriateness of eighteenth-century dress to performances by women on these instruments—

> 'It strikes us ridiculous when we look at a female . . . in a hoop skirt at a double bass; ridiculous when we see her playing the violin with great sleeves flying to and fro; ridiculous when we observe her in a high *fontange* blowing a horn,' affirms our *Almanach* guide. '*Fontange*,' a lofty headdress made of knots of ribbons, was named for a duchess friend of Louis XIV.[3]

With a keyboard instrument, by contrast, a girl could keep

> her feet demurely together, her face arranged into a polite smile or a pleasantly earnest concentration . . . an outward symbol of her family's ability to pay for her education and her decora-

---

3. In Paris, I found a fabulous illustration of costume under Louis XVI. The *pianiste* represented does not have a *fontange*, obviously, but an equally marvelous headdress composed of at least two complete magnolia blooms with foliage. She also plays while wearing gloves that go up to her elbows.

tiveness, of its striving for culture and the graces of life, of its pride in the fact that she did not have to work and that she did not "run after" men.

That said, not every women who played—or was compelled to play—a keyboard instrument in this period was a dilettante. Mozart wrote his first masterpiece, a piano concerto (no. 9, in E-flat, K. 271), for Mademoiselle Jeunehomme—who, if she played this concerto (now named after her) with justice to its wonderment, must have been a remarkable pianist indeed. (Mozart wrote no more beautiful slow movement in any of his concerti.) Haydn wrote his F minor variations for, and dedicated them to, Babette von Ployer (for whom Mozart had written two concerti). He also composed three sonatas—among them the big one in E-flat—for Therese Bartolozzi (*née* Jansen). Dorothea von Ertmann, Sophia Hewitt, and Marie Bigot de Morogues were early exponents of Beethoven's music: Ertmann was the dedicatee of his opus 101 sonata (one of his toughest); Hewitt's 27 February 1819 performance of the opus 26 sonata (one of the movements of which is a funeral march), in Boston, may have been—according to Loesser—"the earliest public hearing of an important Beethoven piano composition in America"; while Bigot de Morogues—in Paris, the teacher of the boy Mendelssohn-Bartholdy—was the first to play the *Appassionata* sonata for the composer himself (from manuscript).

The most obvious fact that McClary seems to ignore is that men arrived on the concert scene first; that music had a "strong traditional association" with men *before* it did with women: Clementi, Cramer (called "Glorious John," he included—unusually for the time—music not written by him on his programs), Dussek, Field (the Irish pianist who was the first to write nocturnes for the piano), Hiller, Hummel (whom Einstein called "the musical idol of the German 'Biedermeier Period,' that age . . . satisfied with elegant polish, pleasant wit, and friendly conversation"), Kalkbrenner (Chopin's idol), Moscheles, Ries, Steibelt (who often appeared with his wife, a tambourinist, in concert), and Josef Wölfl were among the first *virtuosi*. Such pianists were long famous—Beethoven had lived and died, and Liszt had concluded his "Years of Transcendental Execution"—by the time

Charlotte Brontë wrote *Villette* (1853), where she illustrates the still essentially trivial relationship of women to music at the time. Brontë describes a concert in Villette (the novel's eponymous setting) in which the mediocrity of the music making annoys the (female) narrator.

> The young ladies of the Conservatoire, being very much frightened, made rather a tremulous exhibition on the two grand pianos. M. Josef Emanuel stood by them while they played; but he had not the tact or influence of his kinsman, who, under similar circumstances, would certainly have *compelled* pupils of his to demean themselves with heroism and self-possession. M. Paul would have placed the hysteric débutantes between two fires—terror of the audience, and terror of himself—and would have inspired them with the courage of desperation, by making the latter terror incomparably the greater: M. Josef could not do this.

The key here is the word "compelled"; the idea that only an exceptional teacher could have inspired these students to be more than "hysteric débutantes," which irritates the proto-feminist narrator. Yet as Brontë herself might have been the first to profess, true artists need never be compelled; "between two fires," the students do not burn with Pater's "hard, gem-like flame."[4]

In short, it is no coincidence that until the late nineteenth or early twentieth century the majority of paintings that depict someone playing a keyboard instrument show Everywoman. (Clara Schumann was, it appears, the first internationally known female pianist to merit a full-scale portrait in oils; the famous painting of Sophie Menter by Ilya Repin came later.) By contrast, until the same date, a man depicted at a keyboard was nearly always a specific composer or performer: Händel, J. C. Bach (painted by Gainsborough), Mozart, Haydn, Weber, Beethoven, Schubert (Klimt), Chopin (Delacroix's being the most famous),

---

4. Young women who played the piano—as well as the men who taught or listened to them—often burned with another kind of flame. Indeed, one example each from painting and literature will show that piano study sometimes trespassed on the very bourgeois values that it sought to exalt. In Fragonard's "La leçon de musique," a young man is more charmed by a young woman's breasts than by her playing. In Flaubert's *Madame Bovary,* weekly piano lessons are the pretense that allow Emma to go to her lover in Rouen.

and Liszt. Male composers and *virtuosi*, unlike women, were painted not because of their outward beauty: they were painted because art claims the forms of a civilization's virtues.

* * *

Forster's fictional cosmos is an intensely musical one, and Beethoven's music is at its heart. Forster himself played the piano throughout his long life, and this tells in his writing. "Playing Beethoven, as I do generally," he wrote in the essay "Not Listening to Music,"

> I grow familiar with his tricks, his impatience, his sudden softness, his dropping of a tragic theme one semitone, his love, when tragic, for the key of C minor, and his aversion to the key of B major. This gives me a physical approach to Beethoven which cannot be gained through the slough of "appreciation." Even when people play as badly as I do, they should continue: it will help them to listen.

Lucy Honeychurch, the heroine of *A Room with a View*, may be literature's most outstanding woman virtuoso—and she is neither a "professional" nor a competition winner. The penultimate chapter of Hildebrandt's *Pianoforte: A Social History of the Piano* (titled "Accomplice in Catastrophe: The Piano in the Novel of the Nineteenth Century") names several fictions with women piano players that pre-date Forster's novel: Tolstoy's *The Kreutzer Sonata* (an inversion, even perversion, of Forster's views of Beethoven because his music precipitates adultery),[5] Austen's *Emma* and *Pride and Prejudice*, Charlotte Brontë's *Jane Eyre*, Goethe's *Elective Affinities*, Fontane's *Effi Briest*, Flaubert's *Madame Bovary* and Sen-

---

5. Tolstoy, on Beethoven's *Kreutzer* sonata:

... can one really allow it to be played in a drawing-room full of women in low-cut dresses? To be played, and then followed by a little light applause, and the eating of ice-cream, and talk about the latest society gossip? Such pieces should only be played on certain special, solemn, significant occasions when certain solemn actions have to be performed, actions that correspond to the nature of the music.... Otherwise the generation of all that feeling and energy, which are quite inappropriate to either the place or the occasion, and which aren't allowed any outlet, can't have anything but a harmful effect.

timental Education, Edmond and Jules Goncourt's *Renée Mauperin,*
Thackeray's *Vanity Fair,* and Collins's *The Woman in White.* What
makes Lucy superior to them all is that she has access—both lit-
erally and metaphorically—to a wider repertoire than her antecedents.

At the beginning of chapter two, Forster describes the musical scene painted on the ceiling in Lucy's room with a view in the
Pension Bertolini, in Florence: "pink griffins and blue amorini
sport in a forest of yellow violins and bassoons." This atmosphere
contradicts the very essence of Lucy's Romantic temperament—
as, indeed, do her performances of Mozart late in the novel.
Forster is being typically ironic when he writes that Lucy is "no
dazzling executante; her runs were not at all like strings of pearls,
and she struck no more right notes than was suitable for one of
her age and situation." For Lucy really is a virtuoso—it is a condition of the spirit for her (and, indeed, for most artists). She
wants "something big"—even if it is "unladylike" (that is, virtuosic) to the Edwardian sense of the world:

> Why? Why were most big things unladylike? Charlotte had
> once explained to her why. It was not that ladies were inferior
> to men; it was that they were different. Their mission was to in-
> spire others to achievement rather than to achieve themselves.
> Indirectly, by means of tact and a spotless name, a lady could
> accomplish much. But if she rushed into the fray, she would be
> first censured, then despised, and finally ignored. Poems had
> been written to illustrate this point.

Music—especially virtuoso music—externalizes Lucy's interior
experience by giving form to those of her feelings that are imper-
missible at Windy Corner, her home in England. Indeed, Windy
Corner becomes an elegant symbol of the different forces within
Lucy herself (like Schumann's Florestan and Eusebius): she, both
as a woman and as an artist, is "cornered" by England, yet like
the wind she possesses a power that is both transformative and
transcendent.

> Lucy, who found daily life rather chaotic, entered a more solid
> world when she opened the pianoforte. She was then no longer
> either deferential or patronizing; no longer either a rebel or a
> slave. The kingdom of music is not the kingdom of this world.

Lucy's sympathy with the remark of the Miss Alans (spinster sisters staying at Bertolini) that "there are people who do things which are most indelicate, and yet at the same time—beautiful" further testifies to her (latent) Romantic nature. To be sure, "indelicate, and yet at the same time—beautiful" is a credo worthy of Blake.

Lucy's most important performances in *A Room with a View* are of music by Beethoven, then Schumann. Of the former, she plays the last piano sonata rather than (a transcription of) his song *Adelaide* (a setting of a text by Matthisson) that Mr. Beebe expects from her. The vicar at Tunbridge Wells remarks to him that "it is sheer perversity to choose a thing like that, which, if anything, disturbs," but Mr. Beebe, who knows music better than the vicar, also knows that Lucy is giving an extraordinary performance of the sonata. Forster once began an analytical catalogue of the Beethoven sonatas, but did not get to the last one. Failing the presence of his own study, one can turn to Cecil Gray (in his autobiography *Musical Chairs*) to articulate the significance of Beethoven's work to such a character as Lucy:

> Beethoven . . . exemplifies the opposite principle of free-will. He is master of his fate, the captain of his soul. There is no element in his work of divine inevitability. The whole plot can be reversed at a moment's notice, and frequently is, as the outcome of pure willfulness or caprice. The element of the unexpected is paramount. Anything can, and generally does, happen with him.

Barthes elaborates this idea in *Image-Music-Text:*

> Beethoven was the first man of music to be *free*. Now for the first time the fact of having successive *manners* was held to the glory of an artist; he was acknowledged the right of metamorphosis, he could be dissatisfied with himself or, more profoundly, with his language, he could change his codes as he went through life. . . . From this moment that the work becomes the trace of a movement, of a journey, it appeals to the idea of fate. The artist is in search of his 'truth' and this quest forms an order in itself. . . .

(The grand failing of Jane Campion's film *The Piano* is the musical touchstone she gives her piano-playing heroine: not Beethoven, but Michael Nyman.)

Part One of *A Room with a View* is set in Italy, where in a field of violets—"the primal source whence beauty gushed out to water the earth"—Lucy is kissed by George Emerson. Part Two of the novel is set in England, where Lucy becomes engaged to Cecil Vyse (after having rejected his earlier proposals). Cecil's awareness of "culture" is broader and more sophisticated than Lucy's—than all the Honeychurches, and also all the Emersons, in fact—yet as his views on paintings and music and Italy itself attest, he is also academic and snobbish and, as his almost morality-play name implies, suffocating (and suffocated): in the mercantile sense that Steiner points out, he "appreciates" and criticizes, yet all art—even Lucy herself—is for him part of a museum culture. This conflict between the active and the passive culminates in Lucy breaking off the engagement and telling Cecil,

> you may understand beautiful things, but you don't know how to use them; and you wrap yourself up in art and books and music, and would try to wrap me up. I won't be stifled, not by the most glorious music, for people are more glorious, and you hide them from me . . . you were all right as long as you kept to things, but when you came to people—.

Before the engagement has been broken, however, Lucy plays the piano in Cecil's mother's London flat. She chooses Schumann (music of "querulous beauty"), after which Cecil asks her to play Beethoven. Again she plays Schumann.[6] This is her most profound performance in the novel:

> The melody rose, unprofitably magical. It broke; it was resumed broken, not marching once from the cradle to the grave. The sadness of the incomplete—the sadness that is often Life, but should never be Art—throbbed in its dejected phrases, and made the nerves of the audience throb. Not thus had she played on the little draped pianoforte at the Bertolini, and 'Too much Schumann' was not the remark that Mr. Beebe had passed to himself when she returned.

Forster does not say which Schumann work Lucy played, but my detective sense tells me it was the *Grosse Humoreske*, opus 20. Schumann was the first composer to use the title *Humoreske* for

<hr/>

6. In the Merchant-Ivory adaptation of this novel, Lucy here plays Schubert (from the A minor sonata, D. 537).

a musical composition; a title that invokes both rapture and caprice. (Probably not coincidentally, the title of the chapter preceding this performance is "Cecil as Humorist.")

Near the end of *A Room with a View,* Mr. Beebe carries the honors of the day by persuading Mrs. Honeychurch to allow Lucy to travel to Greece (and perhaps Constantinople) with the Miss Alans. Prior to gaining the assent of her mother, however, Mr. Beebe hears Lucy "tinkling at a Mozart Sonata" as he attains the drawing room at Windy Corner and remarks to himself, "how delicate those Sonatas are"—even though "at the bottom of his heart he thought them silly little things." Given Mr. Beebe's (and Forster's) attitude to Mozart—that he did not go so far, and was not as big, as Beethoven—Lucy's playing of his music is regressive. Moreover, it is on this occasion that she plays the ancient air from *The Bride of Lammermoor* (set to music by Henry R. Bishop) that Cecil has given her:

> Look not thou on beauty's charming,—
> Sit thou still when kings are arming,—
> Taste not when the wine cup glistens,—
> Speak not when the people listens,—
> Stop thine ear against the singer,—
> From the red gold keep thy finger,—
> Vacant heart and hand and eye,—
> Easy live and quiet die.

As Lucy herself soon realizes, the silence of the "stopped ear" differs vastly from the one at the end of the novel, when Phaethon's song "die[s] away" and she hears only "the river, bearing down the snows of winter into the Mediterranean." By the end Lucy has managed to clarify her muddle (catharsis in its original sense, as clarification) and thus to fulfill the prophecy that she will live as she plays: she has married George and returned with him to Florence. Having mastered the piano, Lucy has mastered herself: she has proven herself a virtuoso.

16.

Mephistopheles in Soutanes

Mozart has won, since his death in 1791, the laurels as "favorite" or "greatest" composer from Hilaire Belloc, Brahms, Britten, Busoni (whose farewell concerts in Berlin, in 1922, contained the music of Mozart alone: twelve of the piano concerti), Albert Einstein, Gounod, Kierkegaard ("I have [Mozart] to thank that I did not die without having loved"), Lawrence, the old Arthur Rubinstein, Shaw, Tchaikovsky, and Wagner. Moreover, Mozart's music has achieved an unprecedented dissemination: not merely the 180 CDs of Philips's "Mozart Edition," but festivals around the globe—from Lincoln Center's "Mostly Mozart," to Salzburg, to Oklahoma. Further tributes to him include the candies named for him by the confectioners Hofbauer (Mozartkugel), Mirabell, and Paul Reber; Montblanc's miniature version of its classic *Meister-stück* pens and mechanical pencil (accompanied by a compact disc of his music); and the room—nay, the temple—that the parents of a gentleman of my acquaintance placed apart for listening to Mozart's, and only Mozart's, music. (A character in Saki's novel *When William Came: A Story of London under the Hohenzollerns* does the same: "'All the hangings, *violette de Parme,* all the furniture, rosewood. The only ornament in the room is a *replica* of the Mozart statue in Vienna. Nothing but Mozart is to be played in the room. Absolutely, nothing but Mozart'.") Finally, in the visual arts, Chagall and Dufy sought to reflect in paintings the qualities of color, grace, and lyrical motion that they perceived and revered in Mozart's music.

No, in our century, no composer has been quite so globally celebrated as Mozart—in spite of the fact that his contribution to the piano sonata, the string quartet and the symphony was arguably less significant than Haydn's or Beethoven's. (Only in opera and the piano concerto is he head and shoulders above everyone else.) And no composer presents so thorough a paradox: if Mozart is truly the most divine of all composers (when Raphael was still considered the greatest of painters, he was called the "Raphael of Music"), then why is the contemporary desire also to vulgarize him (as, for example, in the play and film *Amadeus*) so keen? No composer inspires less reasoned responses than Mozart.

In 1934, Ernest Newman had considered the historical twinning of Mozart and Raphael, and concluded that comparison to Raphael was no longer the highest compliment that could be paid to the composer, since Salomon Reinach had by then produced the first truly critical study of the painter:

> The worship of Raphael, "the divine painter," has had its day. His works must now be analyzed and judged one by one, not as those of a god in the form of a painter, but as the creations of an artist of genius, fallible like the rest of mankind, and deified by irresponsible enthusiasm. All that is truly great in his art can but gain by being studied critically, not in the spirit of depreciation, but, on the other hand, without a blind determination to admire at any price.

Where Mozart is concerned this "blind determination to admire" still prevails. I happen to admire (although not deify) Mozart; even so, I recognize that those who seize opportunities to knock him off the pedestal upon which others have placed him have a legitimate reason for doing so: Mozart was a flesh-and-blood man, and representations of him as anything other than that are frivolous, and consequently provocative. Mozart's father wanted his son's letters to him to record an exemplary life, but Mozart himself wanted nothing to do with that: he would not be what anyone else would have him be. His letters are endowed with uncommon love and humor, yet they also show his pride and jealousy, his viciousness in judging his colleagues, his greed (he wrote on 4 April 1781 that his "sole aim" was to get as much money as possible).

Two radically different contemporary advertisements use

Mozart in ways that underline our ambivalence toward him. The first, for Platinum MasterCard, reads

> antique baby grand piano: $7,000
> weekly lessons: $75
> vintage metronome:[1] $200
> learning Mozart at 48: priceless

The second, for American Standard toilets, reads, "Plato. Shakespeare. Mozart. They all went to the bathroom." The former is possibly more vulgar than the latter, for even pricelessness is a category of economic valuation—and economic valuation of art is vulgar in a way that shitting can never be.

The traditions according to which we interpret composers' lives, like the ones according to which we interpret their music, have everything to do with our specific, selfish requirements of them. Mozart and his music, rooted as they are in a civilization so different from ours, are seen as proof of the existence of God Himself, or at least of Godly Things. If, for me, Mozart's music is not superior to Schubert's (the supreme proof of Bacon's dictum "There is no beauty that hath not some strangeness in the proportion," or Baudelaire's "Le beau est toujours bizarre"), I recognize that it has nonetheless the properties of the sacred. The very transcendent qualities of his operas are not those of humankind: justice (*Don Giovanni*), forgiveness (*La Clemenza di Tito*), love (*Le Nozze de Figaro*). We want to perform, to practice, to know these things fully, but we cannot, and to assert that human beings are essentially petty and limited—imperfect, in sum—is not to be misanthropic but merely to accept our destiny. (When Steiner told Roger Sessions of Lukacs's argument that Nazism could not have made use of Mozart's music as it did of Wagner's, Sessions replied "by playing the opening bars of the aria of the Queen of the Night in *The Magic Flute*.") Mozart's is the voice of failure.

One work of Mozart's that became specially famous as a con-

---

1. The metronome is useless where Mozart's music is concerned: it was invented about 1812, and patented by J. N. Maelzel in 1815. Mozart, who had by then been dead for almost twenty-five years, consequently gave no metronome indications for any of his works.

sequence of the film adaptation of Peter Shaffer's *Amadeus* was the *Requiem* that he had left unfinished at the time of his death. Mozart's pupil Franz Süssmayr completed the work (the Sanctus and the Benedictus), and in this form it has been most widely performed and recorded with high art (by Bruno Walter, for one). Later, however, the incomplete score, edited by Richard Maunder and recorded by Hogwood, was "restored," because Mozart's music now must be kept apart from anything unworthy of it; from what Forster called "the spot of filth without which the spirit cannot cohere." (Dreary purists are out in force. Though Busoni transcribed the *andantino* from Mozart's "Jeunehomme" concerto for solo piano, I am aware of only three pianists who have performed this transcription: Gunnar Johansen, Petri—both of whom also recorded it—and Enrico Rossi. It is the same with the cadenzas that Busoni, Godowsky, Landowska, Saint-Saëns, and others have written for the piano concerti. Tchaikovsky's *Mozartiana* and Reger's *Variations and Fugue on a Theme of Mozart*—orchestral works—are likewise obscure; the latter even more than the former. These works are further evidence of the isolation from the human community—and musical community—that Mozart must suffer for us.)

The authenticity (in the sense of authorship) of the *Requiem* is more than a musicological concern: the modern need for Mozart may result, in part, from living in a desperately toxic world that could, fathomably, cease to sustain us.[2] Because we shall want to live, we do not want the same Mozart who proclaims faith to complete a mass for the dead; to complete his, much less our, funeral song (*canto funebre*). (A decade before Hiroshima and Nagasaki, Wallace Stevens had invoked the composer in "Mozart, 1935," a poem which, as he wrote in a letter to Ronald Lane Latimer, expressed "the status of the poet in a disturbed society.")

The Romantics in particular had little practical use for Mozart: to them, he was first and foremost the composer of *Don Giovanni*, for, as Stendahl proposed, Mozart's Don Juan—unlike

---

2. A supremely awful irony. In 1998, the Mozarteum in Salzburg was closed after two professors died of leukemia: carcinogens in the construction materials of the new building, or electrical transformers buried in its proximity, have been implicated.

Molière's—"thinks less of *what other people will say....*" Stendahl continues:

> It was in Italy and in the seventeenth century that a Princess said, as she sipped an ice with keen enjoyment of the evening of a hot day: '*What a pity, this is not a sin!*'
> This sentiment forms, in my opinion, the foundation of the character of a Don Juan, and, as we see, the Christian religion is necessary to it.

Although Schumann was ever praiseful of Mozart's music ("It is ever with a sense of awe that I have approached the works of Mozart"), his own has little in common with it. Chopin revered Mozart as well, and this reverence influenced his own pianistic textures. (It is unthinkable, for example, that Chopin could have written his A minor mazurka, opus 17, no. 4, had he not known Mozart's rondo, K. 511.) Liszt expressed his love for Mozart's music most dynamically: he often conducted Mozart, and although he played none of his original piano works during his "Years of Transcendental Execution" (at that time the sonatas were perceived as lacking emotional, let alone intellectual, strength), he did compose a paraphrase (now lost) of *The Magic Flute* overture, transcriptions of part of the *Requiem,* and fantasies on *Don Giovanni* and *The Marriage of Figaro.* (The *Don Giovanni* fantasy is the only Mozart-Liszt piece played with any frequency.) I once asked Slonimsky what he thought of Liszt's transcriptions. He paused a moment, then responded, "I think Mozart would have loved them."

Not only is there an appreciation for the music of Mozart's *Don Giovanni* among the Romantics, there is in their own natures something of Don Juan (and Mozart) himself: they, like he, had no choice but to think less of *what other people will say.*

That the Romantics responded to the demonic quality of Mozart's music was natural, for in the popular imagination of the nineteenth century virtuosity was inseparable from *diablerie.* The achievements of Liszt and Paganini in particular were often attributed to pacts with diabolical forces. (Paganini, to contribute to the myth of his own satanic nature, heightened his apparition-like appearance by wearing blue spectacles and playing a violin rumored to be strung with the gut of a mistress. Liszt, though he took orders of priesthood, was described as "Mephistopheles in a soutane."[3]) One has yet to learn why those who hunger for knowledge and talent must turn to the demonic by default. Why does God offer no rival opportunities upon request? Why does Faust seem easier to emulate than Solomon? Christianity demands the acceptance of one's lot, and only those who do so merit the designation "God-given talent." (Such is the popular perception of Mozart, although there is no reason that his talent might not just as easily have been demonic in origin.) One does not have to read many lives of martyrs and thinkers (Giordano Bruno and Galileo, for instance) to discover that Christianity punishes intellectual and aesthetic enquiry and rewards a certain dull-witted and slavish obedience. This was as intolerable a condition for the Romantics as it was for Mozart himself.

3. Liszt composed a number of works that made a nod to the underworld: four *Mephisto* waltzes, a *Mephisto* polka, a sonata "After a Reading of Dante," a *Faust* and a *Dante* symphony (the first movement of latter of which represents the *Inferno*), and paraphrases from such operas as Gounod's *Faust* and Meyerbeer's *Robert le diable*.

THE ANGEL OF THE MUD

The last decade of our (former) century witnessed the death of the few remaining pianists in the Romantic virtuoso tradition. Sviatoslav Richter was the last to go: he died in Moscow on 1 August 1997, at the age of 82—the last citizen of an old order. Richter had portrayed Liszt in Alexandrov's 1952 film *Le Compositeur Glinka*, and his actual life evoked events of Liszt's.

The fact that he was *"un angelo del fango"* in Florence when the Arno flooded its banks in November 1966 is little known. He is shown, in a rare photograph, lifting books from the oily mud. He also gave ten recitals in Italy—each containing the Liszt sonata—in aid of the flood's victims. In 1838, Liszt had hastened from Italy to Vienna when he learned that the Danube had flooded, and gave eight recitals to aid its victims.

I am grateful that I had the privilege of hearing Richter in concert a handful of times. In the face of this loss of the virtuoso, the memory of his virtuosity is itself a consolation. Richter's playing often made me feel as if my heart were breaking, yet it was really mending it—with the knowledge that someone else was feeling what I feel. The virtuoso tells us that artistic eloquence dignifies human life; that we must make meaning to the best of our knowledge and, if we possess it, faith; that beauty and joy are essential, long before we realize what they mean and what use they will be to us; that because we come into and go out of this world alone, love is the apex of experience. The virtuoso's love—for it is nothing less than that—is for me the fullest and most ecstatic expression of human life.

For the virtuoso, Blake's "Exuberance is Beauty" was, and remains, a credo.

Bibliography

Abdul, Raoul. *Blacks in Classical Music: A Personal History*. New York: Dodd, 1977.

Amadeus. Directed by Milos Forman. Performers include F. Murray Abraham, Tom Hulce, Elizabeth Berridge, Simon Callow, Roy Dotrice, Christine Ebersole, Jeffrey Jones. 1984.

Australian Women's Weekly. [Article on Jorge Bolet.] 23 June 1965.

Badura-Skoda, Eva. *The History of the Pianoforte: A Documentary in Sound* (90-minute VHS video). Bloomington: Indiana University Press, 1999.

Baer, Richard. "Tabatha on the Keyboard," episode of *Bewitched*.

Barbellion, W. N. P. *The Journal of a Disappointed Man*. Harmondsworth, Middlesex: Penguin, 1948.

Barthes, Roland. *Image-Music-Text*. Trans. Stephen Heath. London: Fontana-Collins, 1987.

———. *The Pleasure of the Text*. Trans. Richard Miller. New York: Hill and Wang–Noonday, 1975.

Bauer, Harold. *Harold Bauer: His Book*. New York: Norton, 1948.

The Beast with Five Fingers. Dir. Robert Florey. Perf. Robert Alda, Andrea King, Peter Lorre, Victor Francen, J. Carrol Naish. Warner Bros., 1946.

Benjamin, Walter. *Illuminations*. Ed. and with an intro. by Hannah Arendt. Trans. Harry Zorn. London: Pimlico, 1999. New York: Harcourt Brace & World, 1968.

Benko, Gregor. Letters to the author. July–September 1999.

———. "Josef Hofmann and His Recordings," *International Piano Quarterly* Spring 1999: 12–22.

Benson, E[dward]. F[rederic]. *The Challoners*. London: Heinemann, 1904.

Berlioz, Hector. Memoirs of Hector Berlioz, from 1803 to 1865, comprising his travels in Germany, Italy, Russia, and England. Trans. Rachel (Scott Russell) Holmes and Eleanor Holmes. Annotated and translation revised by Ernest Newman. New York: Dover, 1966.

Bernhard, Thomas. *The Loser*. Trans. Jack Dawson. New York: Knopf, 1991.

The Biography of Leopold de Meyer, Imperial and Royal Court Pianist, by Diploma, to Their Majesties and the Emperors of Austria and Russia. London: Palmer & Clayton, 1845.

Blakeney, E. H., ed., and William Smith, *A Smaller Classical Dictionary.* New York: E. P. Dutton, 1934.

Blickstein, Edward, and Gregor Benko. Incomplete and unpublished manuscript of a biography of Vladimir de Pachmann.

Brendel, Alfred. *Music Sounded Out: Essays, Lectures, Interviews, Afterthoughts.* New York: Noonday-Farrar, 1992.

———. *Musical Thoughts and Afterthoughts.* London: Robson, 1982.

Brewster, Harry. *The Cosmopolites: A Nineteenth-Century Family Drama.* Wilby, Norwich: Michael Russell, 1994.

Brillat-Savarin, Jean-Anthelme. *The Physiology of Taste.* Trans. Anne Drayton. London: Penguin, 1994.

Brodkey, Harold. *Stories in an Almost Classical Mode.* New York: Knopf, 1988.

Brontë, Charlotte. *Villette.* Ed. Margaret Smith and Herbert Rosengarten. Oxford and New York: Oxford University Press [World's Classics series], 1990.

Brook, Donald. *Masters of the Keyboard.* London: Rockliff, 1946.

Cardus, Neville. *Autobiography.* London: Hamish Hamilton, 1984.

———. *Talking of Music.* London: Collins, 1957.

Cazort, Jean E., and Constance Tibbs Hobson. *Born to Play: The Life and Career of Hazel Harrison.* Westport, Conn.: Greenwood, 1983.

Chasins, Abram. *Speaking of Pianist.* 2nd ed. New York: Knopf, 1973.

———, with Villa Stiles. *The Van Cliburn Legend.* Garden City, N.Y.: Doubleday, 1959.

Chopin, Frédéric. *Selected Correspondence of Fryderyk Chopin,* trans. and ed. with additional material and a commentary by Arthur Hedley. New York: McGraw-Hill, 1963.

———. *Correspondance de Frédéric Chopin, édition définitive* (in 3 volumes), collected, edited, annotated, and translated by Bronislas Edouard Sydow, with the assistance of Suzanne Chainaye and Denise Chainaye. Paris: Richard-Masse, 1981.

Chotzinoff, Samuel. *A Little Nightmusic.* New York: Harper, 1964.

Church, Michael. "A View from the Hills" [Interview with Krystian Zimerman]. *BBC Music Magazine* May 1998: 39–41.

Crompton, Louis, ed. *The Great Composers: Reviews and Bombardments by Bernard Shaw.* Berkeley, Los Angeles and London: University of California Press, 1978.

Cziffra, Georges. *Cannons and Flowers: The Memoirs of Georges Cziffra.* Trans. John Hornsby. Hexham, England: APR, 1996.

Debussy, Claude. *Monsieur Croche, The Dilettante Hater.* Trans. B. N. Langdon Davies. New York: Viking, 1928.

Della Corte, Andrea. *L'Interpretazione musicale e gli interpreti*. Torino: UTET [Unione tipografico-editrice torinese], 1951.

Drabble, Margaret. *The Needle's Eye*. New York: Ballantine-Ivy, 1989.

Dubal, David, comp. and ed. *Remembering Horowitz: 125 Pianists Recall a Legend*. New York: Schirmer, 1993.

Duhamel, Georges. *La Musique Consolatrice*. Monaco: Éditions du Rocher, 1944.

Edmundson, Mark. "On the Uses of a Liberal Education." *Harper's Magazine* Sept. 1997: 39–49.

Egorov, Youri. *Fantasies by Bach, Mozart, Chopin, Schumann*. Globe, 1988.

Einstein, Alfred. *Music in the Romantic Era: A History of Musical Thought in the Nineteenth Century*. New York: Norton, 1947.

Eliot, George. *Daniel Deronda*. Ed. Terence Cave. London: Penguin, 1995.

———. *Middlemarch: A Study of Provincial Life*. London: Penguin, 1985.

Eliot, T[homas]. S[tearns]. *Collected Poems*. London: Faber, 1974.

Ewan, David, ed. *Romain Rolland's Essays on Music*. New York: Dover, 1959.

Fay, Amy. *Music Study in Germany*. New York: Dover, 1965.

Fitzgerald, Penelope. "Renewing the Struggle." [Review of *Father of the Bensons: The Life of Edward White Benson, Sometime Archbishop of Canterbury* by Geoffrey Palmer and Noel Lloyd.] *London Review of Books* 18 June 1998: 17.

Flaubert, Gustave. *Madame Bovary: A Story of Provincial Life*. Trans. Alan Russell. London: Penguin, 1950.

Ford, Ford Madox. *The Good Soldier: A Tale of Passion*. New York: Vintage International–Random, 1989.

Forster, E[dward]. M[organ]. *Commonplace Book*. Ed. Philip Gardner. Stanford: Stanford University Press, 1985.

———. *Maurice*. London: Penguin, 1972.

———. *A Room with a View*. Ed. Oliver Stallybrass. London: Penguin, 1990.

———. *Two Cheers for Democracy*. Ed. Oliver Stallybrass. London: Arnold, 1972. [Abinger Edition vol. 11]

Furbank, Philip Nicholas. Letter to the author. 23 July 1995.

Furtwängler, Wilhelm. *Notebooks 1924–54*. Trans. Shaun Whiteside. Ed. Michael Tanner. London: Quartet, 1995.

Godowsky, Leopold. Great Pianists of the 20th Century, Vol. 38. Philips, 1999.

Goethe, Johann Wolfgang von. *Elective Affinities*. Trans. R. J. Hollingdale. London: Penguin, 1971.

———. *Italian Journey* [1786–1788]. Trans. W. H. Auden and Elizabeth Mayer. London: Penguin, 1970.

Gould, Stephen Jay. *Life's Grandeur: The Spread of Excellence from Plato to Darwin*. London: Vintage-Random, 1997.

Graffman, Gary. *I Really Should Be Practicing*. Garden City, N.Y.: Doubleday, 1981.

Gray, Cecil. *Musical Chairs, or Between Two Stools*. London: Hogarth, 1985.

Grover, David S. *The Piano: Its Story from Zither to Grand*. New York: Scribner's, 1978.

Hanslick, Eduard. *Music Criticisms*. Trans. and ed. Henry Pleasants. New York: Dover, 1988.

Haskell, Harry. *The Attentive Listener: Three Centuries of Music Criticism*. London: Faber, 1995.

Heilbut, Anthony. *Exiled in Paradise: German Refugee Artists and Intellectuals in America from the 1930s to the Present*. Berkeley and Los Angeles: University of California Press, 1997.

Hildebrandt, Dieter. *Pianoforte: A Social History of the Piano*. Trans. Harriet Goodman. New York: Braziller, 1988.

Hofmann, Josef. *Piano Playing: With Piano Questions Answered*. New York: Dover, 1976.

Holland, Vyvyan. *Son of Oscar Wilde*. Oxford: Oxford University Press, 1988.

Horowitz, Joseph. *Conversations with Arrau*. New York: Knopf, 1982.

———. *The Ivory Trade: Piano Competitions and the Business of Music*. Boston: Northeastern University Press, 1991.

———. *The Post-Classical Predicament: Essays on Music and Society*. Boston: Northeastern University Press, 1995.

Horowitz, Vladimir. Booklet. *Horowitz at Home*. Deutsche Grammophon, 1987.

Huang, Helen. Booklet. *Mozart and Mendelssohn*. Teldec, 1998.

Hubbard, W. L., ed. *The American History and Encyclopedia of Music: Musical Dictionary*. New York: Irving Squire, 1908.

Huneker, James Gibbons. *Steeplejack*. New York: Scribner's, 1922.

Huvé, Cyril. Booklet. *Chopin Scherzi & Ballades*. EMI, 1992.

Huysmans, J. K. [Joris-Karl]. *Against the Grain*. New York: Dover, 1969.

Isherwood, Christopher. *Berlin Stories*. New York: New Directions, 1963.

Jepson, Barbara. "Stepping out of the Shadow of Cliburn" [on John Browning], *New York Times* 24 October 1993: sect. 2, p. 1.

Johnstone, Arthur. *Musical Criticisms*. Manchester: University Press, 1905.

Kaiser, Joachim. *Great Pianists of Our Time*. Trans. David Wooldridge and George Unwin. London: Allen and Unwin, 1971.

Kallberg, Jeffrey. *Chopin at the Boundaries: Sex, History, and Musical Genre*. Cambridge: Harvard University Press, 1996.

Kentner, Louis. *Piano*. Yehudi Menuhin Music Guide 3. London: Kahn & Averill, 1991.

Kerman, Joseph. *Contemplating Music: Challenges to Musicology*. Cambridge: Harvard University Press, 1985.

Kissin, Evgeny. Letter to the author. 2 October 1994.

Kivy, Peter. *Music Alone: Philosophical Reflections on the Purely Musical Experience*. Ithaca and London: Cornell University Press, 1990.

Kozinn, Alan. Review of Maurizio Pollini recital of 2 November 1998. *New York Times* 4 November 1998: D3.

Kroeger, E. R. "Programs for Schubert Recitals," *The Musician* (Boston, April 1907), vol. 12 (No. 4), p. 177.

Lahee, Henry C. *Famous Pianists of To-day and Yesterday*. Boston: L. C. Page, 1901.

Lawrence, D[avid]. H[erbert]. *Complete Poems*. Ed. Vivian de Sola Pinto and F. Warren Roberts. New York: Penguin [Twentieth-Century Classics series], 1977.

Leavitt, David. "Terra ammucchiata," trans. Giulia Crivelli. Milan: Filarmonica della Scala, 1998 / "Heaped Earth," New York: *Tin House* Vol. 1, No. 2 [1999], pp. 8–12.

Lessona, Michele. *Federico Chopin*. ["I Maestri della Musica" no. 11.] Turin: Arione, n.d.

Liberace. *Liberace: An Autobiography*. New York: Putnam, 1973.

———— and Carol Truax. *Liberace Cooks!: Recipes from His Seven Dining Rooms*. Garden City, N.Y.: Doubleday, 1970.

Liszt, Franz. *Frédéric Chopin*. Trans. Edward N. Waters. New York: Vienna House, 1973.

————. *[An Artist's Journey] Lettres d'un bachelier ès musique 1835–1841*. Trans. Charles Suttoni. Chicago and London: University of Chicago Press, 1989.

Loesser, Arthur. *Men, Women and Pianos: A Social History*. New York: Dover, 1990.

Mann, Thomas. *Death in Venice and Other Tales*. Trans. Joachim Neugroschel. New York: Viking Penguin, 1998.

————. *Doctor Faustus: The Life of the German Composer Adrian Leverkühn as Told by a Friend*. Trans. John E. Woods. New York: Knopf, 1997.

Maugham, W. Somerset. *Six Stories Written in the First Person Singular*. London: Heinemann, 1931.

Mayne, Xavier [pseud. of Edward Prime-Stevenson], ed. *Imre: A Memorandum*. Naples: English Book-Press R. Rispoli, 1906; New York: Arno, 1975.

McClary, Susan. "Constructions of Subjectivity in Schubert's Music." *Queering the Pitch: The New Gay and Lesbian Musicology*. Ed. Philip Brett, Elizabeth Wood, and Gary C. Thomas. New York and London: Routledge, 1994. 205–233.

Mellor, David. "All in Good Time." *Gramophone* Aug. 1994: 20–21.

Milton, John. *Paradise Lost*. Ed. Christopher Ricks. London: Penguin, 1989.

Nabokov, Vladimir. *The Stories of Vladimir Nabokov.* New York: Knopf, 1995.

Nardi, Gregorio. Interview with Lazar Berman. *CD Classica* Sept. 1997: 20–21.

Neuhaus, Heinrich. *The Art of Piano Playing.* Trans. K. A. Leibovitch. London: Kahn & Averill, 1993.

Newman, Ernest. *Essays from the World of Music.* Selected by Felix Aprahamian. London: Calder, 1976.

———. *More Essays from the World of Music.* Selected by Felix Aprahamian. London: Calder, 1976.

Nietzsche, Friedrich. *Beyond Good and Evil: Prelude to a Philosophy of the Future.* Trans. Walter Kaufmann. New York: Vintage, 1989.

Norris, Frank. *The Pit.* New York: Doubleday, Page, 1903.

Nyiregyházi, Ervin. *Nyiregyházi Plays Liszt* [*En Rêve,* ballade no. 2, "Sunt lacrymae rerum—en mode hongrois," *Abschied, Légendes*]. International Piano Archives/Desmar, 1977. [Notes by Gregor Benko.]

———. *Nyiregyházi Plays Liszt* [Hungarian rhapsody no. 3, "Mosonyi's Funeral Procession," *Weinachtsbaum* nos. 1 and 2, *Nuages gris, Hamlet,* "Miserere after Palestrina," "March of the Three Holy Kings" from *Christus,* "Aux cyprès de la Villa d'Este" no. 1]. Columbia Masterworks, 1978. [Notes by Richard Kapp, Harold C. Schonberg and Michael Walsh.]

———. *Nyiregyházi* [Grieg, "Sie tanzt" opus 57, no. 5, "Der Hirtenknabe" opus 54, no. 1, waltz in A minor opus 12, no. 2, and "Heimwärts" opus 62, no. 6; Tchaikovsky, "Warum?" opus 6, no. 5, waltz in A-flat major, and romance in F minor opus 5; Blanchet, *Au jardin du vieux sérail;* Bortkiewicz, *Travel Pictures:* "Poland—Mazurka" "Venetian Gondola Song," "In Spain"]. Columbia Masterworks, 1979. [Notes by Leslie Gerber.]

Oestreich, James B. "A Genius Whose Primary Language Was Music." [Review of Brian Newbould's *Schubert: The Music and the Man.*] *New York Times* 18 April 1997: C33.

Ostwald, Peter. *Glenn Gould: The Ecstasy and Tragedy of Genius.* New York: Norton, 1997.

———. *Schumann: The Inner Voices of a Musical Genius.* Boston: Northeastern University Press, 1985.

Paderewski, Ignace Jan, and Mary Lawton. *The Paderewski Memoirs.* New York: Scribner's, 1938.

Page, Tim, ed. *The Glenn Gould Reader.* New York: Vintage-Random, 1990.

Pater, Walter. *The Renaissance,* 3rd ed. 1888.

The Pearl: A Journal of Facetive and Voluptuous Reading. New York: Ballantine, 1973.

Penrose, James F. "The Genius Was Unwell." [Review of Peter F. Ostwald's *Glenn Gould*]. *The Wall Street Journal* 5 Aug. 1997: A16.

Pincherle, Marc. *The World of the Virtuoso.* Trans. Lucile H. Brockway. New York: Norton, 1963.

Pinsky, Robert. "The Green Piano." *New Yorker,* 15 March 1999: 62–63.

Plato. *Republic.* Trans. Robin Waterfield. Oxford and New York: Oxford University Press [World's Classics series], 1993.

Pogorelich, Ivo. Booklet. *Chopin Recital.* Deutsche Grammophon, 1981.

Pollini, Maurizio. Booklet. *Chopin Études.* Deutsche Grammophon, 1972.

Porter, Andrew. *Musical Events. A Chronicle: 1980–1983.* New York: Summit, 1987.

Pound, Ezra. *Selected Poems 1908–1969.* London: Faber, 1977.

Proust, Marcel. *In Search of Lost Time.* Trans. C. K. Scott Moncrieff and Terence Kilmartin. Rev. D. J. Enright. London: Vintage-Random, 1996.

Ratcliffe, Ronald V. *Steinway.* San Francisco: Chronicle, 1989.

Rattalino, Piero. *Da Clementi a Pollini: Duecento anni con i grandi pianisti.* [Third edition.] Florence: Ricordi/Giunti, 1989.

———. *Piano Recital.* Naples: Pagano, 1992.

———. "Play It Again." Trans. Eric Siegel. Booklet note for *Bis!* Ermitage, 1997.

———. *Storia del pianoforte: lo strumento, la musica, gli interpreti.* [New edition.] Milan: Saggiatore, 1996.

Restout, Denise, ed. and trans., assisted by Robert Hawkins. *Landowska on Music.* New York: Stein and Day, 1964.

Révész, Geza. *The Psychology of a Musical Prodigy.* New York: Harcourt, Brace, 1925; translation of *Erwin Nyiregyhazi: Psychologische Analyse eines musikalisch hervorragenden Kindes* (Leipzig, 1916).

Rolland, Romain. *Jean-Christophe.* Introduction by Louis Auchincloss. New York: Carroll and Graf, 1996. [Reprint of the 1910 edition published by Henry Holt and Company.]

Rosen, Charles. *The Romantic Generation.* Cambridge: Harvard University Press, 1995.

———. "On Playing the Piano." *New York Review of Books,* 21 October 1999: 49–52, 54.

Rostand, Claude. *Liszt.* Trans. John Victor. London: Calder, 1972.

Rubens, Bernice. *Madame Sousatzka.* London: Eyre and Spottiswoode, 1962.

Rubinstein, Arthur. *My Young Years.* New York: Knopf, 1973.

———. *My Many Years.* New York: Knopf, 1980.

Sachs, Harvey. *Rubinstein: A Life.* New York: Grove, 1995.

Sadie, Stanley, ed. *The New Grove Dictionary of Music and Musicians.* 20 vols. London: Macmillan, 1980.

Said, Edward W. *Musical Elaborations.* London: Vintage, 1992.

Saint-Saëns, Charles Camille. *Outspoken Essays on Music.* Trans. Fred Rothwell. London: Kegan; New York: Dutton, 1922.

Saki [Hector Hugh Munro]. *The Complete Saki.* London: Penguin, 1982.

Sándor, György. *On Piano Playing: Motion, Sound and Expression.* New York: Schirmer-Simon, 1995.

Saul, John. *The Sins of the Cities of the Plain, or The Recollections of a Mary-Ann.* London, 1881. [Privately printed.]

Schmidt-Görg, Joseph, and Hans Schmidt, eds. *Ludwig van Beethoven Bicentennial Edition 1770–1970.* Bonn: Beethoven-Archiv; Hamburg: Deutsche Grammophon, 1972.

Schnabel, Artur. *My Life and Music.* New York: Dover; Gerrards Cross, England: Smythe, 1988.

Schonberg, Harold C. *The Great Pianists from Mozart to the Present.* New York: Fireside-Simon, 1987.

———. *Horowitz: His Life and Music.* London: Touchstone-Simon, 1993.

Schumann, Robert. *Schumann on Music: A Selection from the Writings.* Trans. and ed. Henry Pleasants. New York: Dover, 1988.

Seth, Vikram. *An Equal Music.* New York: Broadway, 1999.

Shaw, [George] Bernard. *Music in London 1890–94.* 3 vols. London: Constable, 1932.

Shine. Dir. Scott Hicks. Perf. Geoffrey Rush, Armin Mueller-Stahl, Noah Taylor, Alex Rafalowicz, Sonia Todd, Lynn Redgrave, John Gielgud, Nichols Bell, Googie Withers. Miramax, 1996.

Sincerely Yours. Dir. Gordon Douglas. Perf. Liberace, Joanne Dru, Dorothy Malone, William Demarest, Richard Eyer, Lurene Tuttle. Warner Bros., 1955.

Slenczynska, Ruth, with Ann M. Lingg. *Music at Your Fingertips: Advice for the Artist and Amateur on Playing the Piano.* New York: Da Capo, 1968.

Slonimsky, Nicolas. *A Thing or Two about Music.* New York: Allen, Towne and Heath, 1948. Westport, Conn.: Greenwood, 1972.

Smith, Dave. "Tribute to Ervin Nyiregyházi: A Genius in Seclusion." *Los Angeles Times* 2 April 1978, *Calendar:* 50–51.

Soldati, Mario. *Rami secchi.* Milan: Rizzoli, 1989.

Solomon, Andrew. *A Stone Boat.* London: Faber, 1994.

Solomon, Maynard. "Franz Schubert's 'My Dream.'" *American Imago* 38.2 (1981): 137–154.

———. "Franz Schubert and the Peacocks of Benvenuto Cellini." *19th-Century Music.* 12.3 (Spring 1989): 193–206.

A Song to Remember. Dir. Charles Vidor. Perf. Cornel Wilde, Paul Muni, Merle Oberon, Stephen Bekassy, Nina Foch, George Coulouris, Sig Arno. 1945.

Sontag, Susan. "Notes on 'Camp'" in her *Against Interpretation and Other Essays.* New York: Anchor-Doubleday, 1990.

Sorabji, Kaikhosru Shapurji. *Around Music*. London: Unicorn, 1932.

————. *Collected Published Writings*. 2 vols. Bath, England: Sorabji Archive, 1995.

————. *Mi contra fa: The Immoralisings of a Machiavellian Musician*. London: Porcupine, 1947. [The title comes from the Latin: "*mi contra fa diabolus est*."]

Steiner, George. *Real Presences*. London: Faber, 1989.

Stendahl. *Three Italian Chronicles*. Trans. C. K. Scott-Moncrieff. New York: New Directions, 1991.

Stevens, Wallace. *The Collected Poems*. New York: Vintage-Random, 1990.

Stott, R[aymond]. Toole. *Circus and Allied Arts: A World Biography (1500–1957)*. Derby, England: Harpur.

Stravinsky, Igor. *Poetics of Music: In the Form of Six Lessons*. Trans. Arthur Knodel and Ingolf Dahl. Cambridge, Mass., and London: Harvard University Press, 1970.

Tanasescu, Dragos, and Grigore Bargauanu. *Lipatti*. Trans. Carola Grindea and Anne Goosens. London: Kahn & Averill; White Plains, N.Y.: Pro/Am, 1988.

Taylor, Deems. *The Well Tempered Listener*. New York: Simon and Schuster, 1940.

Taylor, Harold, ed. *Kentner: A Symposium*. London: Kahn & Averill; New York: Pro/Am, 1987

Teleny. London: Gay Men's Press, 1986.

Thomas, Bob. *Liberace: The True Story*. London: Weidenfeld, 1987.

Thompson, Wendy, with Fanny Waterman. *Piano Competition: The Story of the Leeds*. London: Faber, 1991.

Thomson, Virgil. *The Musical Scene*. New York: Greenwood, 1968.

Tolstoy, Leo. *The Kreutzer Sonata and Other Stories*. Trans. David McDuff. London: Penguin Classics, 1983.

Tommasini, Anthony. *Virgil Thomson: Composer on the Aisle*. New York: Norton, 1997.

Tournier, Michel. *The Fetishist*. Trans. Barbara Wright. Garden City, N.Y.: Doubleday, 1984.

Tovey, Donald Francis. *Essays in Musical Analysis: Chamber Music*. Oxford: Oxford University Press, 1944.

Van den Toorn, Pieter C. *Music, Politics, and the Academy*. Berkeley and Los Angeles: University of California Press, 1995.

Volodos, Arcadi. Booklet. *Live at Carnegie Hall: October 21, 1998*. Sony, 1999.

Walker, Alan. *Franz Liszt: The Final Years 1861–1886*. New York: Knopf, 1996.

————. *Franz Liszt: The Virtuoso Years 1811–1847*. New York: Knopf, 1990.

————. *Franz Liszt: The Weimar Years 1848–1861*. Ithaca, N.Y.: Cornell University Press, 1993.

Westermayr, Leonhard. *Carl Filtsch* [First World Recording], *Thalberg, Chopin, Liszt.* MMS-Sipario, 1994.

White, Michael. "The Greatest Pianist of His Generation?" *The Independent on Sunday* 9 June 1996.

Wilde, Oscar. *The Portable Oscar Wilde*, rev. ed. Ed. Richard Aldington and Stanley Weintraub. New York: Penguin, 1981.

Zayas, Juana. Booklet. *Chopin Études.* Music and Arts, 1995.

Index

Bigot de Morogues, Marie, 159
Bilotti, Anton, 30
Bishop, Henry R., 165
Blake, William, 47, 173
Blanchet, Emile-Robert, 74
Blumenfeld, Felix, 67
Boegner, Michèle, 35
Böhm, Karl, 92
Bolet, Jorge, 85, 110
Borge, Victor, 120
Bortkiewicz, Sergei, 74
Bossuet, Jacques-Bénige, 8
Boulez, Pierre, 29, 86
Boyd, William, 96
Brahms, Johannes, 17, 39, 85, 118, 124,
    167; performances by, 35, 62, 99;
    performances of works by, 11, 30,
    47, 65, 67, 68, 140; recordings of
    works by, 70, 86; as part of reper-
    toire, 20, 29
Brendel, Alfred, 11–13 passim, 15, 27,
    28, 47, 56, 81, 116, 154
Brett, Philip, 113
Brillat-Savarin, Anthelme, 55
Britten, Benjamin, 19, 92, 167
Brontë, Charlotte, 160, 161
Browning, John, 110, 141
Bruno, Giordano, 172
Busch Quartet, 12
Busoni, Ferruccio, 57, 128, 143, 167;
    performances of works by, 66, 155;
    as part of repertoire, 46; transcrip-
    tions and editions by, 3, 18, 24–25,
    63, 73, 170
Butts, Mary, 25
Byrd, William, 21

Campion, Jane, 163
Caramiello, Francesco, 57
Cardus, Neville, 23, 34, 76, 134
Carnegie Hall, 13, 29, 48, 63, 66, 73,
    89, 119, 120, 141, 147
Carpenter, Edward, 114
Carreño, Teresa, 72
Carter, Elliott, 92
Casadesus, Gaby, 91
Cascioli, Gianluca, 38, 57
Casella, Alfredo, 19
Chabrier, Emmanuel, 55

Chagall, Marc, 167
Chaminade, Cécile, 55
Chantavoine, Jean, 77
Chasins, Abram, 20, 46, 109, 139, 140
Cherkassky, Shura, 133
Cherubini, Luigi, 92
Chicago Symphony Orchestra, 86, 119
Chopin, Frédéric (Fryderyk): life and
    ideas of, 16, 59, 69, 114, 159, 171; in
    literature, film, and material cul-
    ture, 36, 75, 76, 91, 96, 98, 99, 102,
    120, 122, 124–126, 160; perfor-
    mances of works by, 10, 13, 24, 33,
    48, 62, 63, 64, 65, 66, 73, 79, 89, 145,
    151, 152, 155; reception of, 17–18,
    25, 34, 45, 47, 49–50, 93, 116; record-
    ings of works by, 2, 6, 22, 31, 35, 61,
    92, 156; as part of repertoire, 11, 14,
    29, 46, 140; transcriptions, editions,
    reworkings of works by, 19, 36, 57
Chotzinoff, Samuel, 111
Church, Michael, 153
Ciani, Dino, 57
Ciccolini, Aldo, 55
Clementi, Muzio, 46, 57, 119, 141, 159
Cleveland Orchestra, 30, 141
Cliburn, Van (Harvey Lavan, Jr.),
    109–110, 139–141, 148
Cohen, Patrick, 35
Collins, Wilkie, 162
Conroy, Frank, 96
Cooper, Frank, 18
Corigliano, John, 117
Cortot, Alfred, 6, 22, 30, 35, 39, 56,
    128, 140, 147
Couperin, François, 33, 70
Cowan, Robert, 153
Cramer, John, 46, 159
Cristina Trivulzio principessa di
    Belgioioso, 27
Cristofori, Bartolomei, 59
Curzon, Sir Clifford, 7, 140
Czerny, Carl, 14, 21, 46, 59, 65
Cziffra, György, 28, 76, 106

d'Albert, Eugène, 20
Dalberto, Michel, 19
Damerini, Massimiliano, 57
Dang Thai Son, 148

MARK MITCHELL

edited *The Penguin Book of International Gay Writing,* and, with David Leavitt, co-edited selected stories by E. M. Forster for Penguin Twentieth-Century Classics (forthcoming), *Pages Passed from Hand to Hand: The Hidden Tradition of Homosexual Literature in English from 1748 to 1914,* and *The Penguin Book of Gay Short Stories.* He wrote an introduction to the Elysium Press edition of William Plomer's "Local Colour" and, again with Leavitt, co-authored *Italian Pleasures.* His writing has appeared in the *New York Times Book Review, Papers on Language and Literature,* and *The Southwest Review,* among other publications. He is currently writing a biography of Vladimir de Pachmann.